RESUMES
FOR
RE-ENTERING
THE
JOB MARKET

Professional Resumes Series

RESUMES
FOR
RE-ENTERING
THE
JOB MARKET

The Editors of VGM Career Books

Second Edition, with Sample Cover Letters

VGM Career Books

Chicago New York San Francisco Lisbon London Madrid Mexico City
Milan New Delhi San Juan Seoul Singapore Sydney Toronto

Library of Congress Cataloging-in-Publication Data

Resumes for re-entering the job market / the editors of VGM Career Books. — 2nd ed.,
with sample cover letters.
      p.   cm. — (VGM professional resumes series)
  ISBN 0-07-138731-5
  1. Resumes (Employment).   2. Employment re-entry.   I. VGM Career Books (Firm).
  II. Series.
    HF5383 .R448   2002
  650.14'2—dc21

                                                      2002019979

VGM Career Books

A Division of The McGraw·Hill Companies

The editors gratefully acknowledge the assistance of Megan Phillips in the compiling and
editing of this book.

1 2 3 4 5 6 7 8 9 0 VLP/VLP 1 0 9 8 7 6 5 4 3 2

ISBN 0-07-138731-5

This book was set in Minion by Ellen Kollmon
Printed and bound by Vicks Lithograph

This book is printed on acid-free paper.

Contents

Introduction

Your resume is a piece of paper (or an electronic document) that serves to introduce you to the people who will eventually hire you. To write a thoughtful resume, you must thoroughly assess your personality, your accomplishments, and the skills you have acquired. The act of composing and submitting a resume also requires you to carefully consider the company or individual that might hire you. What are they looking for, and how can you meet their needs? This book shows you how to organize your personal information and experience into a concise and well-written resume, so that your qualifications and potential as an employee will be understood easily and quickly by a complete stranger.

Writing the resume is just one step in what can be a daunting job-search process, but it is an important element in the chain of events that will lead you to your new position. While you are probably a talented, bright, and charming person, your resume may not reflect these qualities. A poorly written resume can get you nowhere; a well-written resume can land you an interview and potentially a job. A good resume can even lead the interviewer to ask you questions that will allow you to talk about your strengths and highlight the skills you can bring to a prospective employer. Even a person re-entering the job market after a lengthy break can find a good job if he or she is assisted by a thoughtful and polished resume.

Lengthy, typewritten resumes are a thing of the past. Today, employers do not have the time or the patience for verbose documents; they look for tightly composed, straightforward, action-based resumes. Although a one-page resume is the norm, a two-page resume may be warranted if you have had extensive job experience or have changed careers and truly need the space to properly position yourself. If, after careful editing, you still need more than one page to present yourself, it's acceptable to use a second page. A crowded resume that's hard to read would be the worst of your choices.

Distilling your work experience, education, and interests into such a small space requires preparation and thought. This book takes you step-by-step through the process of crafting an effective resume that will stand out in today's competitive marketplace. It serves as a workbook and a place to write down your experiences, while also including the techniques you'll need to pull all the necessary elements together. In the following pages, you'll find many examples of resumes that are specific to re-entering the job market. Study them for inspiration and find what appeals to you. There are a variety of ways to organize and present your information; inside, you'll find several that will be suitable to your needs. Good luck landing the job of your dreams!

Chapter 1

The Elements of an Effective Resume

An effective resume is composed of information that employers are most interested in knowing about a prospective job applicant. This information is conveyed by a few essential elements. The following is a list of elements that are found in most resumes—some essential, some optional. Later in this chapter, we will further examine the role of each of these elements in the makeup of your resume.

- Heading
- Objective and/or Keyword Section
- Work Experience
- Education
- Honors
- Activities
- Certificates and Licenses
- Publications
- Professional Memberships
- Special Skills
- Personal Information
- References

The first step in preparing your resume is to gather information about yourself and your past accomplishments. Later you will refine this information, rewrite it using effective language, and organize it into an attractive layout. But first, let's take a look at each of these important elements individually so you can judge their appropriateness for your resume.

Heading

Although the heading may seem to be the simplest section of your resume, be careful not to take it lightly. It is the first section your prospective employer will see and it contains the information she or he will need to contact you. At the very least, the heading must contain your name, your home address, and, of course, a phone number where you can be reached easily.

In today's high-tech world, many of us have multiple ways that we can be contacted. You may list your E-mail address if you are reasonably sure the employer makes use of this form of communication.

If you have voice mail or a reliable answering machine, list its number in the heading and make sure your greeting is professional and clear. Always include at least one phone number in your heading, even if it is a temporary number, where a prospective employer can leave a message.

You might have a dozen different ways to be contacted, but you do not need to list all of them. Confine your numbers or addresses to those that are the easiest for the prospective employer to use and the simplest for you to retrieve.

Objective

When seeking a specific career path, it is important to list a job or career objective on your resume. This statement helps employers know the direction you see yourself taking, so they can determine whether your goals are in line with those of their organization and the position available. Normally, an objective is one to two sentences long. Its contents will vary depending on your career field, goals, and personality. The objective can be specific or general, but it should always be to the point. See the sample resumes in this book for examples.

If you are planning to use this resume online, or you suspect your potential employer is likely to scan your resume, you will want to include a "keyword" in the objective. This allows a prospective employer, searching hundreds of resumes for a specific skill or position objective, to locate the keyword and find your resume. In essence, a keyword is what's "hot" in your particular field at a given time. It's a buzzword, a shorthand way of getting a particular message across at a glance. For example, if you are a lawyer, your objective might state your desire to work in the area of corporate litigation. In this case, someone searching for the keyword "corporate litigation" will pull up your resume and know that you want to plan, research, and present cases at trial on behalf of the corporation. If your objective states that you "desire a challenging position in systems design," the keyword is "systems design," an industry-specific, shorthand way of saying that you want to be involved in assessing the need for, acquiring, and implementing high-technology systems. These are keywords and every industry has them, so it's becoming more and more important to include a few in your resume. (You may need to conduct additional research to make sure you know what keywords are most likely to be used in your desired industry, profession, or situation.)

There are many resume and job-search sites online. Like most things in the online world, they vary a great deal in quality. Use your discretion. If you plan to apply for jobs online or advertise your availability this way, you will want to design a scannable resume. This type of resume uses a format that can be easily scanned into a computer and added to a database. Scanning allows a prospective employer to use keywords to quickly review each applicant's experience and skills, and (in the event that there are many candidates for the job) to keep your resume for future reference.

Many people find that it is worthwhile to create two or more versions of their basic resume. You may want an intricately designed resume on high-quality paper to mail or hand out *and* a resume that is designed to be scanned into a computer and saved on a database or an online job site. You can even create a resume in ASCII text to E-mail to prospective employers. For further information, you may wish to refer to the *Guide to Internet Job Searching*, by Frances Roehm and Margaret Dikel, updated and published every other year by VGM Career Books, a division of the McGraw-Hill Companies. This excellent book contains helpful and detailed information about formatting a resume for Internet use. To get you started, in Chapter 3 we have included a list of things to keep in mind when creating electronic resumes.

Although it is usually a good idea to include an objective, in some cases this element is not necessary. The goal of the objective statement is to provide the employer with an idea of where you see yourself going in the field. However, if you are uncertain of the exact nature of the job you seek, including an objective that is too specific could result in your not being considered for a host of perfectly acceptable positions. If you decide not to use an objective heading in your resume, you should definitely incorporate the information that would be conveyed in the objective into your cover letter.

Work Experience

Work experience is arguably the most important element of them all. Your education, if recent, or your former positions will provide the central focus of the resume. You will want this section to be as complete and carefully constructed as possible. By thoroughly examining your work experience, you can get to the heart of your accomplishments and present them in a way that demonstrates and highlights your qualifications.

If you left the job market to go to school, your resume will probably focus on your education, but you should also include information on your previous work or volunteer experiences. Although you will have less information about work experience than a person who has held multiple positions or is advanced in his or her career, the amount of information is not what is most important in this section. How the information is presented and what it says about you as a worker and a person is what really counts.

As you create this section of your resume, remember the need for accuracy. Include all the necessary information about each of your jobs, including your job title, dates of employment, name of your employer, city, state, responsibilities, special projects you handled, and accomplishments. Be sure to list only accomplishments for which you were directly responsible. And don't be alarmed if you haven't participated in or worked on special projects, because this section may not be relevant to certain jobs.

The most common way to list your work experience is in *reverse chronological order*. In other words, start with your most recent experience and work your way backward. If you are re-entering the same field, your last position may be the most important and should be listed first. If it's the most important in terms of responsibilities and relevance to the job for which you are applying, it should also be the one that includes the most information as compared to your previous positions.

The following worksheet is provided to help you organize your experiences in the working world. It will also serve as an excellent resource to refer to when updating your resume in the future.

WORK EXPERIENCE

Job One:

Job Title _____

Dates _____

Employer _____

City, State _____

Major Duties _____

_____

_____

_____

_____

_____

_____

_____

Special Projects _____

_____

_____

_____

Accomplishments _____

_____

_____

_____

_____

_____

_____

Job Two:

Job Title _____

Dates _____

Employer _____

City, State _____

Major Duties _____

_____

_____

_____

_____

_____

_____

Special Projects _____

_____

_____

_____

Accomplishments _____

_____

_____

_____

_____

_____

_____

_____

Job Three:

Job Title _____

Dates _____

Employer _____

City, State _____

Major Duties _____

_____

_____

_____

_____

_____

_____

_____

Special Projects _____

_____

_____

_____

Accomplishments _____

_____

_____

_____

_____

_____

_____

_____

Job Four:

Job Title _____

Dates _____

Employer _____

City, State _____

Major Duties _____

_____

_____

_____

_____

_____

_____

_____

_____

Special Projects _____

_____

_____

_____

Accomplishments _____

_____

_____

_____

_____

_____

_____

_____

_____

Education

Education is usually the second most important element of a resume. Your educational background is often a deciding factor in an employer's decision to interview you. Highlight your accomplishments in school as much as you did those accomplishments at work. If you have just completed a degree, your education may be your greatest asset. In this case, the education section becomes the most important means of selling yourself.

Include in this section all the degrees or certificates you have received; your major or area of concentration; all of the honors you earned; and any relevant activities you participated in, organized, or chaired. Again, list your most recent schooling first. If you have completed graduate-level work, begin with that and work your way back through your undergraduate education. If you have completed college, you generally should not list your high school experience; do so only if you earned special honors, you had a grade point average that was much better than the norm, or this was your highest level of education.

If you have completed a large number of credit hours in a subject that may be relevant to the position you are seeking, but did not obtain a degree, you may wish to list the hours or classes you completed. Keep in mind, however, that you may be asked to explain why you did not finish the program. If you are currently in school, list the degree, certificate, or license you expect to obtain and the projected date of completion.

The following worksheet will help you gather the information you need for this section of your resume.

EDUCATION

School One _____

Major or Area of Concentration _____

Degree _____

Dates _____

School Two _____

Major or Area of Concentration _____

Degree _____

Dates _____

Honors

If you include an honors section in your resume, you should highlight any awards, honors, or memberships in honorary societies that you have received. (You may also incorporate this information into your education section.) Often, the honors are academic in nature, but this section also may be used for special achievements in sports, clubs, or other school activities. Always include the name of the organization awarding the honor and the date(s) received. Use the following worksheet to help you gather your information.

HONORS

Honor One _____

Awarding Organization _____

Date(s) _____

Honor Two _____

Awarding Organization _____

Date(s) _____

Honor Three _____

Awarding Organization _____

Date(s) _____

Honor Four _____

Awarding Organization _____

Date(s) _____

Honor Five _____

Awarding Organization _____

Date(s) _____

Activities

Perhaps you were active in different organizations or clubs during your years at school; often an employer will look at such involvement as evidence of initiative, dedication, and good social skills. Examples of your ability to take a leading role in a group should be included on a resume, if you can provide them. (Information about your activities also may be incorporated into your education section.) If you have been out of school for some time, the activities section of your resume can present neighborhood and community activities, volunteer positions, and so forth. In general, you may want to avoid listing any organization whose name indicates the race, creed, sex, age, marital status, sexual orientation, or nation of origin of its members because this could expose you to discrimination. Use the following worksheet to list the specifics of your activities.

ACTIVITIES

Organization/Activity _____

Accomplishments _____

_____

_____

Organization/Activity _____

Accomplishments _____

_____

_____

Organization/Activity _____

Accomplishments _____

_____

_____

As your work experience grows through the years, your school activities and honors will carry less weight and be emphasized less in your resume. Eventually, you will probably list only your degree and any major honors received. As time goes by, your job performance and the experience you've gained become the most important elements in your resume, which should change to reflect this.

Certificates and Licenses

If your chosen career path requires specialized training, you may already have certificates or licenses. You should list these if the job you are seeking requires them and you, of course, have acquired them. If you have applied for a license but have not yet received it, use the phrase "application pending."

License requirements vary by state. If you have moved or are planning to relocate to another state, check with that state's board or licensing agency for all licensing requirements.

Always make sure that all of the information you list is completely accurate. Locate copies of your certificates and licenses, and check the exact date and name of the accrediting agency. Use the following worksheet to organize the necessary information.

CERTIFICATES AND LICENSES

Name of License _____

Licensing Agency _____

Date Issued _____

Name of License _____

Licensing Agency _____

Date Issued _____

Name of License _____

Licensing Agency _____

Date Issued _____

Publications

Some professions strongly encourage or even require that you publish. If you have written, coauthored, or edited any books, articles, professional papers, or works of a similar nature that pertain to your field, you will definitely want to include this element. Remember to list the date of publication and the publisher's name, and specify whether you were the sole author or a coauthor. Book, magazine, or journal titles are generally italicized, while the titles of articles within a larger publication appear in quotes. (Check with your reference librarian for more about the appropriate way to present this information.) For scientific or research papers, you will need to give the date, place, and audience to whom the paper was presented.

Use the following worksheet to help you gather the necessary information about your publications.

PUBLICATIONS

Title and Type (Note, Article, etc.) _____

Title of Publication (Journal, Book, etc.) _____

Publisher _____

Date Published _____

Title and Type (Note, Article, etc.) _____

Title of Publication (Journal, Book, etc.) _____

Publisher _____

Date Published _____

Title and Type (Note, Article, etc.) _____

Title of Publication (Journal, Book, etc.) _____

Publisher _____

Date Published _____

Professional Memberships

Another potential element in your resume is a section listing professional memberships. Use this section to describe your involvement in professional associations, unions, and similar organizations. It is to your advantage to list any professional memberships that pertain to the job you are seeking. Many employers see your membership as representative of your desire to stay up-to-date and connected in your field. Include the dates of your involvement and whether you took part in any special activities or held any offices within the organization. Use the following worksheet to organize your information.

PROFESSIONAL MEMBERSHIPS

Name of Organization _____

Office(s) Held_____

Activities _____

Dates _____

Name of Organization _____

Office(s) Held_____

Activities _____

Dates _____

Name of Organization _____

Office(s) Held_____

Activities _____

Dates _____

Name of Organization _____

Office(s) Held_____

Activities _____

Dates _____

Special Skills

The special skills section of your resume is the place to mention any special abilities you have that relate to the job you are seeking. You can use this element to present certain talents or experiences that are not necessarily a part of your education or work experience. Common examples include fluency in a foreign language, extensive travel abroad, or knowledge of a particular computer application. "Special skills" can encompass a wide range of talents, and this section can be used creatively. However, for each skill you list, you should be able to describe how it would be a direct asset in the type of work you're seeking, because employers may ask just that in an interview. If you can't think of a way to do this, it may be extraneous information.

Personal Information

Some people include personal information on their resumes. This is generally not recommended, but you might wish to include it if you think that something in your personal life, such as a hobby or talent, has some bearing on the position you are seeking. This type of information is often referred to at the beginning of an interview, when it may be used as an "icebreaker." Of course, personal information regarding your age, marital status, race, religion, or sexual orientation should never appear on your resume as *personal information*. It should be given only in the context of memberships and activities, and only when doing so would not expose you to discrimination.

References

References are not usually given on the resume itself, but a prospective employer needs to know that you have references who may be contacted if necessary. All you need to include is a single sentence at the end of the resume: "References are available upon request," or even simply, "References available." Have a reference list ready—your interviewer may ask to see it! Contact each person on the list ahead of time to see whether it is all right for you to use him or her as a reference. This way, the person has a chance to think about what to say *before* the call occurs. This helps ensure that you will obtain the best reference possible.

Writing Your Resume

Now that you have gathered the information for each section of your resume, it's time to write it out in a way that will get the attention of the reviewer—hopefully, your future employer! The language you use in your resume will affect its success, so you must be careful and conscientious. Translate the facts you have gathered into the active, precise language of resume writing. You will be aiming for a resume that keeps the reader's interest and highlights your accomplishments in a concise and effective way.

Resume writing is unlike any other form of writing. Although your seventh-grade composition teacher would not approve, the rules of punctuation and sentence building are often completely ignored. Instead, you should try for a functional, direct writing style that focuses on the use of verbs and other words that imply action on your part. Writing with action words and strong verbs characterizes you to potential employers as an energetic, active person, someone who completes tasks and achieves results from his or her work. Resumes that do not make use of action words can sound passive and stale. These resumes are not effective and do not get the attention of any employer, no matter how qualified the applicant. Choose words that display your strengths and demonstrate your initiative. The following list of commonly used verbs will help you create a strong resume:

administered	assembled
advised	assumed responsibility
analyzed	billed
arranged	built

carried out	inspected
channeled	interviewed
collected	introduced
communicated	invented
compiled	maintained
completed	managed
conducted	met with
contacted	motivated
contracted	negotiated
coordinated	operated
counseled	orchestrated
created	ordered
cut	organized
designed	oversaw
determined	performed
developed	planned
directed	prepared
dispatched	presented
distributed	produced
documented	programmed
edited	published
established	purchased
expanded	recommended
functioned as	recorded
gathered	reduced
handled	referred
hired	represented
implemented	researched
improved	reviewed

saved	supervised
screened	taught
served as	tested
served on	trained
sold	typed
suggested	wrote

Let's look at two examples that differ only in their writing style. The first resume section is ineffective because it does not use action words to accent the applicant's work experiences:

WORK EXPERIENCE
Regional Sales Manager

Manager of sales representatives from seven states. Manager of twelve food chain accounts in the East. In charge of the sales force's planned selling toward specific goals. Supervisor and trainer of new sales representatives. Consulting for customers in the areas of inventory management and quality control.

Special Projects: Coordinator and sponsor of annual food industry sales seminar.

Accomplishments: Monthly regional volume went up 25 percent during my tenure while, at the same time, a proper sales/cost ratio was maintained. Customer-company relations were improved.

In the following paragraph, we have rewritten the same section using action words. Notice how the tone has changed. It now sounds stronger and more active. This person accomplished goals and really *did* things.

WORK EXPERIENCE
Regional Sales Manager

Managed sales representatives from seven states. Oversaw twelve food chain accounts in the eastern United States. Directed the sales force in planned selling toward specific goals. Supervised and trained new sales representatives. Counseled customers in the areas of inventory management and quality control. Coordinated and sponsored the annual Food Industry Seminar. Increased monthly regional volume 25 percent and helped to improve customer–company relations during my tenure.

One helpful way to construct the work experience section is to make use of your actual job descriptions—the written duties and expectations your employers had for a person in your former position. Job descriptions are rarely written in proper resume language, so you will have to rework them, but they do include much of the information necessary to create this section of your resume. If you have access to job descriptions for your former positions, you can use the details to construct an action-oriented paragraph. Often, the human resources department can provide a job description for your former position.

The following is an example of a typical human resources job description, followed by a rewritten version of the same description employing action words and specific details about the job. Again, pay attention to the style of writing instead of the content, as the details of your own experience will be unique.

WORK EXPERIENCE
Public Administrator I

Responsibilities: Coordinate and direct public services to meet the needs of the nation, state, or community. Analyze problems; work with special committees and public agencies; recommend solutions to governing bodies.

Aptitudes and Skills: Ability to relate to and communicate with people; solve complex problems through analysis; plan, organize, and implement policies and programs. Knowledge of political systems, financial management, personnel administration, program evaluation, and organizational theory.

WORK EXPERIENCE
Public Administrator I

Wrote pamphlets and conducted discussion groups to inform citizens of legislative processes and consumer issues. Organized and supervised 25 interviewers. Trained interviewers in effective communication skills.

After you have written out your resume, you are ready to begin the next important step: assembly and layout.

Chapter 3

Assembly and Layout

At this point, you've gathered all the necessary information for your resume and rewritten it in language that will impress your potential employers. Your next step is to assemble the sections in a logical order and lay them out on the page neatly and attractively to achieve the desired effect: getting the interview.

Assembly

The order of the elements in a resume makes a difference in its overall effect. Clearly, you would not want to bury your name and address somewhere in the middle of the resume. Nor would you want to lead with a less important section, such as special skills. Put the elements in an order that stresses your most important accomplishments and the things that will be most appealing to your potential employer. For example, if you recently graduated from school, you will want the reviewer to read about your education before any previous jobs that did not require your new degree. If you were gainfully employed for several years and held an important position in your company, you should list your work accomplishments ahead of your educational information, which has become less pertinent with time.

Certain things should always be included in your resume, but others are optional. The following list shows you which are which. You might want to use it as a checklist to be certain that you have included all of the necessary information.

Essential	**Optional**
Name	Cellular Phone Number
Address	Pager Number
Phone Number	E-Mail Address or Website Address
Work Experience	Voice Mail Number
Education	Job Objective
References Phrase	Honors
	Special Skills
	Publications
	Professional Memberships
	Activities
	Certificates and Licenses
	Personal Information
	Graphics
	Photograph

Your choice of optional sections depends on your own background and employment needs. Always use information that will put you in a favorable light—unless it's absolutely essential, avoid anything that will prompt the interviewer to ask questions about your weaknesses or something else that could be unflattering. Make sure your information is accurate and truthful. If your honors are impressive, include them in the resume. If your activities in school demonstrate talents that are necessary for the job you are seeking, allow space for a section on activities. If you are applying for a position that requires ornamental illustration, you may want to include border illustrations or graphics that demonstrate your talents in this area. If you are answering an advertisement for a job that requires certain physical traits, a photo of yourself might be appropriate. A person applying for a job as a computer programmer would *not* include a photo as part of his or her resume. Each resume is unique, just as each person is unique.

Types of Resumes

So far we have focused on the most common type of resume—the *reverse chronological* resume—in which your most recent job is listed first. This is the type of resume usually preferred by those who have to read a large number of resumes, and it is by far the most popular and widely circulated. However, this style of presentation may not be the most effective way to highlight *your* skills and accomplishments.

If you are reentering the workforce after many years or are trying to change career fields, the *functional* resume may work best. This type of resume puts the focus on your achievements instead of the sequence of your work history. In the functional resume, your experience is presented through your general accomplishments and the skills you have developed in your working life.

A functional resume is assembled from the same information you gathered in Chapter 1. The main difference lies in how you organize the information. Essentially, the work experience section is divided in two, with your job duties and accomplishments constituting one section and your employers' names, cities, and states; your positions; and the dates employed making up the other. Place the first section near the top of your resume, just below your job objective (if used), and call it *Accomplishments* or *Achievements*. The second section, containing the bare essentials of your work history, should come after the accomplishments section and can be called *Employment History* since it is a chronological overview of your former jobs.

Since you are reentering the workforce after a long absence, a functional resume is the obvious choice. The identities of previous employers (who aren't part of your new career field) need to be downplayed. And if you lack full-time work experience, you will need to draw attention away from this fact and put the focus on your skills and abilities. You may need to highlight your volunteer activities and part-time work. Education may also play a more important role in your resume.

The other sections of your resume remain the same. The work experience section is the only one affected in the functional format. By placing the section that focuses on your achievements at the beginning, you draw attention to these achievements. This puts less emphasis on whom you worked for and when, and more on what you did and what you are capable of doing.

The type of resume that is right for you will depend on your personal circumstances. It may be helpful to create both types and then compare them. Which one presents you in the best light? Examples of both types of resumes are included in this book. Use the sample resumes in Chapter 5 to help you decide on the content, presentation, and look of your own resume.

Special Tips for Electronic Resumes

Because there are many details to consider in writing a resume that will be posted or transmitted on the Internet, or one that will be scanned into a computer when it is received, we suggest that you refer to the *Guide to Internet Job Searching*, by Frances Roehm and Margaret Dikel, as previously mentioned. However, here are some brief, general guidelines to follow if you expect your resume to be scanned into a computer.

- Use standard fonts in which none of the letters touch.

- Keep in mind that underlining, italics, and fancy scripts may not scan well.

- Use boldface and capitalization to set off elements. Again, make sure letters don't touch. Leave at least a quarter inch between lines of type.

- Keep information and elements at the left margin. Centering, columns, and even indenting may change when the resume is optically scanned.

- Do not use any lines, boxes, or graphics.

- Place the most important information at the top of the first page. If you use two pages, put your name and "Page 2 of 2" at the top of the second page.

- List each telephone number on its own line in the header.

- Use multiple keywords or synonyms for what you do to make sure your qualifications will be picked up if a prospective employer is searching for them. Use nouns that are keywords for your profession.

- Be descriptive in your titles. For example, don't just use "assistant"; use "legal office assistant."

- Make sure the contrast between print and paper is good. Use a high-quality laser printer and white or very light-colored 8½-by-11-inch paper.

- Mail a high-quality laser print or an excellent copy. Do not fold or use staples, as this might interfere with scanning. You may, however, use paper clips.

In addition to creating a resume that works well for scanning, you may want to have a resume that can be E-mailed to reviewers. Because you may not know what word processing application the recipient uses, the best format to use is ASCII text. (ASCII stands for "American Standard Code for Information Exchange.") It allows people with very different software platforms to exchange and understand information. (E-mail operates on this principle.) ASCII is a simple, text-only language, which means you can include only simple text. There can be no use of boldface, italics, or even paragraph indentations.

To create an ASCII resume, just use your normal word processing program; when finished, save it as a "text only" document. You will find this option under the "save" or "save as" command. Here is a list of things to *avoid* when crafting your electronic resume:

- Tabs. Use your space bar. Tabs will not work.

- Any special characters, such as mathematical symbols.

- Word wrap. Use hard returns (the return key) to make line breaks.

- Centering or other formatting. Align everything at the left margin.

- Bold or italic fonts. Everything will be converted to plain text when you save the file as a "text only" document.

Check carefully for any mistakes before you save the document as a text file. Spellcheck and proofread it several times, then ask someone with a keen eye to go over it again for you. Remember: the key is to keep it simple. Any attempt to make this resume pretty or decorative may result in a resume that is confusing and hard to read. After you have saved the document, you can cut and paste it into an E-mail or onto a website.

Layout for a Paper Resume

A great deal of care—and much more formatting—is necessary to achieve an attractive layout for your paper resume. There is no single appropriate layout that applies to every resume, but there are a few basic rules to follow in putting your resume on paper:

- Leave a comfortable margin on the sides, top, and bottom of the page (usually one to one and a half inches).

- Use appropriate spacing between the sections (two to three line spaces are usually adequate).

- Be consistent in the *type* of headings you use for different sections of your resume. For example, if you capitalize the heading EMPLOY-MENT HISTORY, don't use initial capitals and underlining for a section of equal importance, such as <u>Education</u>.

- Do not use more than one font in your resume. Stay consistent by choosing a font that is fairly standard and easy to read, and don't change it for different sections. Beware of the tendency to try to make your resume original by choosing fancy type styles; your resume may end up looking unprofessional instead of creative. Unless you are in a very creative and artistic field, you should almost always stick with tried-and-true type styles like Times New Roman and Palatino, which are often used in business writing. In the area of resume styles, conservative is usually the best way to go.

- Always try to fit your resume on one page. If you are having trouble with this, you may be trying to say too much. Edit out any repetitive or unnecessary information, and shorten descriptions of earlier jobs where possible. Ask a friend you trust for feedback on what seems unnecessary or unimportant. For example, you may have included too many optional sections. Today, with the prevalence of the personal computer as a tool, there is no excuse for a poorly laid-out resume. Experiment with variations until you are pleased with the result.

CHRONOLOGICAL RESUME

JENNIE LYNN BLOOM

132 Palm Court • San Pedro, CA • Work: 310/555-1267 • Pager: 310/555-8772

OBJECTIVE

To seek a position as a sales representative for a fitness/exercise company.

SUMMARY OF QUALIFICATIONS

- Aspire to successful achievements in my chosen field as a sales representative.
- Extremely fitness minded and health conscious.
- Possess a bodybuilding physique that defines muscularity and femininity.
- Enjoy competing on the dais as well as in career-oriented situations.
- Relate to people personally regardless of whether or not their philosophy coincides with mine.

AWARDS & ACHIEVEMENTS

- First runner-up for Ms. Southern California bodybuilding contest, Los Angeles, 2001.
- Second runner-up for Ms. Laguna Beach Bunny competition, Laguna Beach, 2000.
- Semifinalist contestant in the "American Gladiators" television series competition, Hollywood, 1999.
- Received second-place trophy for mixed-pairs posing-routine competition held in Atlanta, 1998.
- Awarded first-place crown for Ms. San Diego Natural Physique contest, San Diego, 1997.

EMPLOYMENT

Gold's Gym/Santa Monica, California
Personal Trainer, part-time, 1996 - 2000. Worked closely with a variety of clients. Researched and applied fitness regiments specialized for each client

Vic Tanny's Vitamin World, Inc./Los Angeles, California
Sales Clerk, 1995 - 1998. Assisted customers in vitamin and health food selections.

Dunham's Sport World/Santa Monica, California
Sales Clerk, 1993 - 1995. Helped customers in purchasing weight training equipment, workout attire, and sports clothes. Assisted in setting up new store locations in Southern California. Helped train new sales staff clerks.

EDUCATION

UCLA/Riverside campus
B.S. in Physical Education, Degree awarded 1993.

International Sports Sciences Association/Santa Barbara
Fitness Trainer Certification, 1997.

References available upon request.

FUNCTIONAL RESUME

CAROL SCHMIDT
12 Overlook Drive
Pager: (303) 555-4467
Denver, Colorado 88021
cschmidt@xxx.com

OBJECTIVE

To seek a position as a travel consultant within a travel facility with opportunities for advancement.

PROFESSIONAL EXPERIENCE

Lufthansa German Airlines
Los Angeles, California
Reservation Sales, 1995 - 1999
Provided travel arrangement reservations for passengers. Computed international fares and taxes; secured hotel and car reservations; arranged sale of ticket with credit card, travel agency, or airline ticket office. Working knowledge of the Siemans and Amadeus computer program system. Training course successfully completed in Germany: Advanced Reservations, Psychology in Sales, and Quality in Daily Work.

South African Airways
San Francisco, California
Customer Service Reservation Sales, 1992 - 1995
Booked international reservations using the Safari computer program system, with passengers, tour operators, wholesale consolidators, and travel agents. Courses successfully completed: Effective Sales Techniques in Reservations, Johannesburg, South Africa. International Fare Calculation, New York City.

Premier Travel Agency
Denver, Colorado
Travel Agent, 1989 - 1992
Booked vacation and corporate travel reservations for clients on the phone and in person including hotel, car, cruise ship, and rail reservations.

EDUCATION

Atlantic Travel Agents School, Kansas City, Kansas
Certification, 1989
Comprehensive training in all phases of air, land, and sea reservation-booking transactions. Manual and computer fare calculation, ticket issue, agency accounting systems, and general office duties.

Remember that a resume is not an autobiography. Too much information will only get in the way. The more compact your resume, the easier it will be to review. If a person who is swamped with resumes looks at yours, catches the main points, and then calls you for an interview to fill in some of the details, your resume has already accomplished its task. A clear and concise resume makes for a happy reader and a good impression.

There are times when, despite extensive editing, the resume simply cannot fit on one page. In this case, the resume should be laid out on two pages in such a way that neither clarity nor appearance is compromised. Each page of a two-page resume should be marked clearly: the first should indicate "Page 1 of 2," and the second should include your name and the page number, for example, "Julia Ramirez—Page 2 of 2." The pages should then be stapled together. You may use a smaller font (in the same font as the body of your resume) for the page numbers. Place them at the bottom of page one and the top of page two. Again, spend the time now to experiment with the layout until you find one that looks good to you.

Always show your final layout to other people and ask them what they like or dislike about it, and what impresses them most when they read your resume. Make sure that their responses are the same as what you want to elicit from your prospective employer. If they aren't the same, you should continue to make changes until the necessary information is emphasized.

Proofreading

After you have finished typing the master copy of your resume and before you have it copied or printed, thoroughly check it for typing and spelling errors. Do not place all your trust in your computer's spellcheck function. Use an old editing trick and read the whole resume backward—start at the end and read it right to left and bottom to top. This can help you see the small errors or inconsistencies that are easy to overlook. Take time to do it right because a single error on a document this important can cause the reader to judge your attention to detail in a harsh light.

Have several people look at the finished resume just in case you've missed an error. Don't try to take a shortcut; not having an unbiased set of eyes examine your resume now could mean embarrassment later. Even experienced editors can easily overlook their own errors. Be thorough and conscientious with your proofreading so your first impression is a perfect one.

We have included the following rules of capitalization and punctuation to assist you in the final stage of creating your resume. Remember that resumes often require use of a shorthand style of writing that may include sentences without periods and other stylistic choices that break the standard rules of grammar. Be consistent in each section, and throughout the whole resume, with your choices.

RULES OF CAPITALIZATION

- Capitalize proper nouns, such as names of schools, colleges, and universities; names of companies; and brand names of products.

- Capitalize major words in the names and titles of books, tests, and articles that appear in the body of your resume.

- Capitalize words in major section headings of your resume.

- Do not capitalize words just because they seem important.

- When in doubt, consult a manual of style such as *Words into Type* (Prentice-Hall) or *The Chicago Manual of Style* (The University of Chicago Press). Your local library can help you locate these and other reference books. Many computer programs also have grammar help sections.

RULES OF PUNCTUATION

- Use commas to separate words in a series.

- Use a semicolon to separate series of words that already include commas within the series. (For an example, see the first rule of capitalization.)

- Use a semicolon to separate independent clauses that are not joined by a conjunction.

- Use a period to end a sentence.

- Use a colon to show that examples or details follow that will expand or amplify the preceding phrase.

- Avoid the use of dashes.

- Avoid the use of brackets.

- If you use any punctuation in an unusual way in your resume, be consistent in its use.

- Whenever you are uncertain, consult a style manual.

Putting Your Resume in Print

You will need to buy high-quality paper for your printer before you print your finished resume. Regular office paper is not good enough for resumes; the reviewer will probably think it looks flimsy and cheap. Go to an office supply store or copy shop and select a high-quality bond paper that will make a good first impression. Select colors like white, off-white, or possibly a light gray. In some industries, a pastel may be acceptable, but be sure the color and feel of the paper makes a subtle, positive statement about you. Nothing in the choice of paper should be loud or unprofessional.

If your computer printer does not reproduce your resume properly and produces smudged or stuttered type, either ask to borrow a friend's or take your disk (or a clean original) to a printer or copy shop for high-quality copying. If you anticipate needing a large number of copies, taking your resume to a copy shop or a printer is probably the best choice.

Hold a sheet of your unprinted bond paper up to the light. If it has a watermark, you will want to point this out to the person helping you with copies; the printing should be done so that the reader can read the print and see the watermark the right way up. Check each copy for smudges or streaks. This is the time to be a perfectionist—the results of your careful preparation will be well worth it.

The Cover Letter

Once your resume has been assembled, laid out, and printed to your satisfaction, the next and final step before distribution is to write your cover letter. Though there may be instances where you deliver your resume in person, you will usually send it through the mail or online. Resumes sent through the mail always need an accompanying letter that briefly introduces you and your resume. The purpose of the cover letter is to get a potential employer to read your resume, just as the purpose of the resume is to get that same potential employer to call you for an interview.

Like your resume, your cover letter should be clean, neat, and direct. A cover letter usually includes the following information:

1. Your name and address (unless it already appears on your personal letterhead) and your phone number(s); see item 7.

2. The date.

3. The name and address of the person and company to whom you are sending your resume.

4. The salutation ("Dear Mr." or "Dear Ms." followed by the person's last name, or "To Whom It May Concern" if you are answering a blind ad).

5. An opening paragraph explaining why you are writing (for example, in response to an ad, as a follow-up to a previous meeting, at the suggestion of someone you both know) and indicating that you are interested in whatever job is being offered.

6. One or more paragraphs that tell why you want to work for the company and what qualifications and experiences you can bring to the position. This is a good place to mention some detail about

that particular company that makes you want to work for them; this shows that you have done some research before applying. It is also a good place to explain your hiatus from the job market—pursued an advanced degree, spent more time with children, etc.

7. A final paragraph that closes the letter and invites the reviewer to contact you for an interview. This can be a good place to tell the potential employer which method would be best to use when contacting you. Be sure to give the correct phone number and a good time to reach you, if that is important. You may mention here that your references are available upon request.

8. The closing ("Sincerely" or "Yours truly") followed by your signature in a dark ink, with your name typed under it.

Your cover letter should include all of this information and be no longer than one page in length. The language used should be polite, businesslike, and to the point. Don't attempt to tell your life story in the cover letter; a long and cluttered letter will serve only to annoy the reader. Remember that you need to mention only a few of your accomplishments and skills in the cover letter. The rest of your information is available in your resume. If your cover letter is a success, your resume will be read and all pertinent information reviewed by your prospective employer.

Producing the Cover Letter

Cover letters should always be individualized because they are always written to specific individuals and companies. Never use a form letter for your cover letter or copy it as you would a resume. Each cover letter should be unique, and as personal and lively as possible. (Of course, once you have written and rewritten your first cover letter until you are satisfied with it, you can certainly use similar wording in subsequent letters. You may want to save a template on your computer for future reference.) Keep a hard copy of each cover letter so you know exactly what you wrote in each one.

There are sample cover letters in Chapter 6. Use them as models or for ideas of how to assemble and lay out your own cover letters. Remember that every letter is unique and depends on the particular circumstances of the individual writing it and the job for which he or she is applying.

After you have written your cover letter, proofread it as thoroughly as you did your resume. Again, spelling or punctuation errors are a sure sign of carelessness, and you don't want that to be a part of your first impression on a prospective employer. This is no time to trust your spellcheck function. Even after going through a spelling and grammar check, your cover letter should be carefully proofread by at least one other person.

Print the cover letter on the same quality bond paper you used for your resume. Remember to sign it, using a good, dark-ink pen. Handle the letter and resume carefully to avoid smudging or wrinkling, and mail them together in an appropriately sized envelope. Many stores sell matching envelopes to coordinate with your choice of bond paper.

Keep an accurate record of all resumes you send out and the results of each mailing. This record can be kept on your computer, in a calendar or notebook, or on file cards. Knowing when a resume is likely to have been received will keep you on track as you make follow-up phone calls.

About a week after mailing resumes and cover letters to potential employers, contact them by telephone. Confirm that your resume arrived and ask whether an interview might be possible. Be sure to record the name of the person you spoke to and any other information you gleaned from the conversation. It is wise to treat the person answering the phone with a great deal of respect; sometimes the assistant or receptionist has the ear of the person doing the hiring.

You should make a great impression with the strong, straightforward resume and personalized cover letter you have just created. We wish you every success in securing the career of your dreams!

Sample Resumes

This chapter contains dozens of sample resumes for people seeking to re-enter the job market in a wide variety of jobs and careers in the field of information services, or who have had experience in this field in the past.

There are many different styles of resumes in terms of layout and presentation of information. These samples also represent people with varying amounts of education and work experience. Model your resume after these samples. Choose one resume or borrow elements from several different resumes to help you construct your own.

GERRY ROBINSON

1012 Edward Ave.
Palisades Park, NJ 07020
E-mail: gerryrobinson@xxx.com
201-555-3942

OBJECTIVE
To work as a dog and cat groomer.

EDUCATION
Nash Academy of Animal Arts, Cliffside Park, NJ
Trained in grooming all breeds of dogs and cats.
Certificate, 2001

Palisades Park High School
Palisades Park, NJ
Diploma, 1992

WORK EXPERIENCE
Bill's Pet Shop, Englewood, NJ
Assistant Manager: Duties included maintaining a running inventory on all pet supplies and executing sales to customers. 1992 - 1995

VOLUNTEER
Teterboro Animal Shelter, Teterboro, NJ
Devote one day a week to caring for the animals placed in the shelter. 1995 - Present.

RELATED ACTIVITIES
Have inaugurated a monthly newsletter containing information on animals who are looking for homes. This project was started in 1994 and has a distributorship of more than 100 businesses and offices in the northern New Jersey area. During this time, more than 300 animals have been placed in homes as a result.

SUMMARY OF QUALIFICATIONS
I have a high regard for all animals and enjoy working with the different breeds of dogs and cats. I especially feel rewarded after professionally grooming them and knowing they feel great too.

REFERENCES
Available upon request.

RENA A. MADISON
1412 Bittersweet Court
Roanoke, VA 23059

Objective: *Seeking a position as a seamstress.*

Education: LISA MARTELL SCHOOL OF CLOTHING DESIGN
Roanoke, VA, Certificate Awarded 1986
Course studies included the successful completion of
Pattern Designing, Pattern Grading, and Pattern Making.
Accomplished sewing of seasonal clothing for adults and
children.

Work Experience: **Marvel Dry Cleaners**
Roanoke, VA
SEAMSTRESS, 1995 - 2000
Duties: Altered and repaired customer clothing.

Elaine's Boutique
Roanoke, VA
ASSISTANT SEAMSTRESS, 1988 - 1995
Duties: Assisted head seamstress in altering ladies' fine
apparel.

New Frocks Fabric Store
Roanoke, VA
SALES CLERK, 1986 - 1988
Duties: Assisted customers in selections of fabric and
accessories. Made cash and credit card sales
transactions. Oversaw inventory control.

Related Activities: Assistant instructor of the adult education course "Learning to Sew It Right," at Wilford High School each spring
and fall semester since 1998.

Have designed and made custom fashions for friends and
family.

Hobbies: Quilting. Designing and making costumes for different
events of the year: Halloween, school plays, and theme
parties.

References: *Available upon request.*

JULIA M. JOHNSDOTTIR

222 Barnaby Ave.
Wheatland, PA 19451
215-555-1234
Johnsdottir@xxx.com

OBJECTIVE
A position as a Dental Hygienist in a dental clinic.

EDUCATION
Oldenburg School of Dental Hygiene/Wheatland, PA
A.S. in Dental Hygiene, 2000
Studies included: Chemistry, Radiology, Periodontology, Pathology, Dental Equipment, Oral Embiology, Pharmacology, Anatomy, Nutrition, and Psychology.

LICENSURE
Pennsylvania Dental Hygiene License
National Board Dental Hygiene Exam -- Written, 93
N.E.R.B. Dental Hygiene Exam -- Clinical, 90; Written, 94

CAREER EXPERIENCE
South Salem Dental Clinic/South Salem, PA
Dental Assistant, OJT 1993 - 1996
Duties: Assisted in preparation of patients for dental surgery, recording their blood pressure and temperature. Advised patients regarding medication prescriptions. Sterilized equipment. Oversaw inventory control, ordered supplies, maintained client files for checkup notices.

RELATED EXPERIENCE
Volunteer for Western Pennsylvania Dental Association each year in providing instruction for proper oral hygiene through good dental cleaning habits since 1994 during National Dental Week at local elementary schools.

MEMBERSHIP
Society of Dental Hygienists, 2000 - present

REFERENCES
Furnished upon request.

Marie M. Patterson
33 Wrigley Avenue, Apt. 22
Hyattstown, MD 22314

CAREER OBJECTIVE
To utilize my expertise in office management and my administrative abilities.

EXPERIENCE
Office Manager/Secretary, 1990 - 1998
David M. Kartling, M.D., Hyattstown, MD
Duties: Responsible for scheduling appointments for patients, accounts payable and receivable, office payroll, and supervising two part-time receptionists. Compiled the quarterly patient newsletter and interviewed personnel.

Executive Secretary, 1985 - 1990
ADQ Security Systems, Olney, MD
Duties: Executive secretary to the Vice President.

Secretary, 1983 - 1985
U.S. Civil Service Commission Headquarters,
Argentia Defense Force, Argentia, Newfoundland
Duties: Secretary to the Assistant Chief of Staff, Logistics. Typed monthly statistical reports, supply requisitions, and purchase orders.

EDUCATION
Terlane Secretarial School 1981 - 1983
Terlane, MD
Diploma: Studies included office procedures, speed writing, word processing, payroll and billing, and general office management.

ORGANIZATIONS
National Secretaries Alliance
Local Chapter #34; Hyattstown, MD
Office Held: Vice President 1978 - 1981

Sigma Delta Psi
National Business Sorority of Working Professionals
Offices Held: Treasurer 1981 - 1983
Secretary 1983 - 1986

ADDITIONAL SKILLS
Working knowledge of Microsoft Word, Excel, and PowerPoint; Lotus 1-2-3; and Windows.

REFERENCES
Available upon request.

Kathleen A. Johnson

223 Homestead Ave.
Euclid, Ohio 44112
Home: 216/555-9234
Pager: 216/555-7273

Objective
A position in nursing in a hospital/health care facility.

Education
Middletown Memorial Hospital School of Nursing
Middletown, CT
Diploma: 1990

Work Experience
Metropolitan Nurses Temps, Inc., Euclid, OH
1997 - 1999
- Performed duties of primary nursing care.
- Cared for anesthetized patients after surgery.
- Assisted in maternity and geriatric units.

Qualifications
- Volunteered and worked in the field of health care in medical facilities for 7 years following my graduation from nursing school.
- Able to work under pressure in a variety of stressful circumstances.

Related Activities
- Relief nurse covering for nurses on vacation.
- Assisted in teaching CPR at the local YWCA for lifeguard certification.
- Participated in Euclid High School Career Day as member of nursing profession.

Organizations
Active member of the Volunteer Ambulance Corps of Euclid.
Member of the F.O.E., Ladies Auxiliary

Office held: Vice President 1995 - 1997

References
Available upon request.

Jane M. Michaels

12 Harvard Avenue, Apt. G
Reno, NV 72367
702-555-9956
J_Michaels@xxx.com

Objective

An assistant accounting position with opportunities for advancement.

Education

Brighton College, Blairsville, NV 1986 - 1990
Major: Business

Work Experience

Sam's Club department store, Blairsville, NV
Accounting Assistant: 1995 - 1999
Duties: Maintained accounts payable and receivable records. Executed a modified version of the existing accounts payable filing system that increased efficiency by 15 percent. Developed a charge card system for employee purchases that eliminated a business transaction by deducting the payment from the employee's paycheck.

Bell's Landscaping Service, Tartan, NV
Accounting Clerk: 1991 - 1995
Duties: Maintained accounts payable and receivable files. Responsible for the monthly payroll ledger and twice-weekly bank deposits.

Summary of Qualifications

- Excellent interpersonal and communication skills.
- Proficient in handling a variety of tasks concurrently.
- Easily adapt to new procedures and concepts.

Computer Skills

Excel, Lotus 1-2-3, Windows, Solomon General Ledger

References

Furnished upon request.

MELLISSA R. PARKER

3330 Lyndale Avenue
Lockwood, ND 52388
Home: 701/555-9976
Cellular: 701/555-8766

OBJECTIVE

To secure a position as an assistant librarian with the opportunity for advancement to librarian.

EDUCATION

Heathmore College, Heathmore, ND
B.S. in Library Science, 1980
Honors: Dean's List, 1978 - 1990

WORK EXPERIENCE

Fargo Public Library, Fargo, ND
Assistant Librarian, 1993 - 1999
Directed the part-time staff. Maintained an orderly and efficient study atmosphere. Gave guided tours of the library's period decor rooms.

Crandall Public High School, Crandall, ND
Assistant Librarian, 1983 - 1993
Supervised the use of AV equipment by students. Instructed students in the correct use of computer card catalogue reference information.

RELATED EXPERIENCE

Volunteer as school librarian two days a week at Crestview Junior High School, Lockwood, NJ.
Assist students in accessing information. Coordinate with faculty in procuring current AV study aids.

Organized and coordinated a used book sale for the fund drive for the new Horatio Alger wing addition to the Lockwood Public Library in 1999.

INTERPERSONAL SKILLS

Encouraging students to read for enjoyment and learning.
Teaching them the value of keeping a daily journal.

REFERENCES

Available upon request.

CARMELLA MADEROS

4008 Puget Sound Drive • Seattle, WA 98789
206/555-3116 • cm71@xxx.com

CAREER OBJECTIVE

To obtain a position as a court reporter and to utilize my past experience in the legal and administrative field.

EDUCATION

Stenographic Technical Business School, Seattle
Court Reporting, Certification received in September 2000
Two-year curriculum included Court Reporting Procedures and Technology, English Grammar, Legal Terminology, Anatomy and Medical Terminology.

Olympia School of Secretarial Studies, Olympia
Diploma, May 1990
Courses included Word Processing, Speed-Typing, Shorthand, Transcription, Office Procedures, Bookkeeping, Communication Skills, and Basic Computer Course.

WORK EXPERIENCE

Payne and DelaRosa, Attorneys at Law, Bellevue   Secretary/Receptionist, 1994 - 1998
Typed correspondence, coordinated appointments for clients, recorded accounts receivable and payable entries.

Department of Motor Vehicles, Seattle   Clerk, 1990 - 1994
Reissued vehicle registration forms, processed car dealership registrations, issued driver's licenses, and conducted written driver's license tests to Spanish-speaking applicants.

SPECIAL SKILLS

Fluent Spanish
Computer experience -- Lotus and Microsoft Office Suite

MEMBERSHIPS

National Court Reporters Association, NCRA, 2000
Spanish Society of Seattle since 1988
Offices held:
Secretary -- 1985
Vice President -- 1993 & 1994.

REFERENCES
Furnished upon request.

JENNIE LYNN BLOOM

132 Palm Court • San Pedro, CA • Work: 310/555-1267 • Pager: 310/555-8772

OBJECTIVE

To seek a position as a sales representative for a fitness/exercise company.

SUMMARY OF QUALIFICATIONS

- Aspire to successful achievements in my chosen field as a sales representative.
- Extremely fitness minded and health conscious.
- Possess a bodybuilding physique that defines muscularity and femininity.
- Enjoy competing on the dais as well as in career-oriented situations.
- Relate to people personally regardless of whether or not their philosophy coincides with mine.

AWARDS & ACHIEVEMENTS

- First runner-up for Ms. Southern California bodybuilding contest, Los Angeles, 2001.
- Second runner-up for Ms. Laguna Beach Bunny competition, Laguna Beach, 2000.
- Semifinalist contestant in the "American Gladiators" television series competition, Hollywood, 1999.
- Received second-place trophy for mixed-pairs posing-routine competition held in Atlanta, 1998.
- Awarded first-place crown for Ms. San Diego Natural Physique contest, San Diego, 1997.

EMPLOYMENT

Gold's Gym/Santa Monica, California
Personal Trainer, part-time, 1996 - 2000. Worked closely with a variety of clients. Researched and applied fitness regiments specialized for each client

Vic Tanny's Vitamin World, Inc./Los Angeles, California
Sales Clerk, 1995 - 1998. Assisted customers in vitamin and health food selections.

Dunham's Sport World/Santa Monica, California
Sales Clerk, 1993 - 1995. Helped customers in purchasing weight training equipment, workout attire, and sports clothes. Assisted in setting up new store locations in Southern California. Helped train new sales staff clerks.

EDUCATION

UCLA/Riverside campus
B.S. in Physical Education, Degree awarded 1993.

International Sports Sciences Association/Santa Barbara
Fitness Trainer Certification, 1997.

References available upon request.

Louisa Martin-Brooks

1212 Riverton Road • Berkeley, NC 27694 • Cellular: 704-555-6349

Objective

A position in fitness instruction whereby aerobic and weight training counseling will enhance and strengthen a client's body and self-esteem.

Education

The Broadmoor School of Health, Nutrition and Exercise
Centerville, NC
Diploma: 1991

Mountain Lakes Personal Trainer School
Pinewood, NC
Personal Trainer Certification: 2001

Professional Experience

Jack LaLanne Health Spa, Raleigh, NC, 1995 - 1997
Manager, Exercise Instructor
Duties: Taught classes in stretching, calisthenics, and aerobics. Scheduled all classes for the program year and assisted in interviewing class instructors.

YWCA, Raleigh, NC, 1991 - 1993
Exercise Instructor
Duties: Organized developmental youth aerobic programs for children with handicaps. Organized seasonal programs of exercise and social activities for children and adults.

Related Activities

- Coordinated an aerobic program for handicapped adults in conjunction with the Hillside Therapy and Rehabilitation Hospital.
- Designed a low-impact aerobic program for senior citizens under the auspices of the Senior Citizen Organization of Raleigh County.
- Promoted a "Workout Week" on weight training for teenagers, sponsored by the Youth Division of Social Services of Raleigh County.

References: Furnished upon request.

ROBERT LOUIS OSBORNE
47 Tyler Way
Phoenix, AZ 87932
(602) 555-3339

CAREER OBJECTIVE

To be an active member of a dedicated team, providing management, accounting, personnel administration and/or training services to a quality-oriented company or organization.

PROFESSIONAL EXPERIENCE

Contracted Business Administrative Services
Maintain office at residence, 1996 - present.

Provide full charge accounting services through to balance sheet. Offer financial consulting services for local organizations and individuals on a limited contract basis. Services include staff training, development of computer skills, preparation and filing of government and state tax returns and payroll documents.

Utilize 486-DX-66, CD-ROM technology with ACCPAC, QUATTRO PRO, MICROSOFT WORD, LOTUS 1-2-3, WORDSTAR (Advanced), MEDTEC (HEALTH TECH.), MICROSOFT PUBLISHER, MICROSOFT ACCESS, MICROSOFT POWERPOINT, POWER UP, INSTANT ARTIST, CALENDAR CREATOR

1993 - 1996
Phoenix General Hospital, Phoenix, Arizona
Medical Office Management Director

Responsibility and accountability for a staff of nine full-time and four part-time employees.

1986 - 1993
Lancet Consulting Service, Orlando, Florida
Manager

Provided financial and personnel management services to local businesses including clients in medical practices, home furnishings, automobile companies, and service organizations.

1964 - 1986
U.S. Government
Administrative Specialist

Conducted extensive administrative, management, and personnel services to commands with up to 2,500 personnel. Personally accountable and responsible for department budget up to $150,000.

Page 1 of 2

EDUCATION

University of Delaware, Wilmington, Delaware
B.S. in Economics, Diploma 1963
Major: Economics, GPA 3.7
Minor: Accounting

SPECIALIZED TRAINING

Management by Objective (MBO), 1993
Trained in business plan development; subject addressed specific tasks, completion dates, personnel requirements, and cost factors. Goal setting for the work place, division or firm, all meeting overall objectives of management.

Equal Opportunity Employment, 1990
Workshop skills in dealing with personnel from varied backgrounds and ethnic groups. Trained for the evaluation of specific job requirements, to ensure all personnel are treated equally in the employment/promotion process.

Affirmative Action and Human Relations, 1989
Trained to ensure goals are equal for all within the work place environment.

COMMUNITY ACTIVITIES

- Editor and publisher of Tyler Way News, a monthly newsletter advising residents of local events and to unify the Neighborhood Watch Association.
- Homeowners Association, President, 1998
- Big Brothers Association, 1994 - present

REFERENCES

Furnished upon request.

Myrna J. Myers

1786 Starlight Drive
Newton, MA 05342
Home: 617/555-8932
Pager: 617/555-3112

OBJECTIVE
To obtain an entry-level position in public relations.

EDUCATION
Bachelor of Science in Business Administration, 1990
Holister State University
Holister, Massachusetts
Major: Public Relations
GPA 3.2

WORK EXPERIENCE
The Meteor Weekly, Langdon, Massachusetts
Advertising Sales Representative 1992 - 1996
>   Responsible for a sales territory consisting of more than 200,000 people.
>   Conducted sales canvassing with local merchants, and once sale was made,
>   followed the development of the ad until publication.

The Suntel Communications Co., Langdon, Massachusetts
Receptionist and Advertising Media Assistant 1990 - 1992
>   Greeted and received clients; scheduled appointments for advertising
>   account representatives on sales leads.

CAREER RELATED ACTIVITIES
Cochairperson for the annual Early American Cultural Festival for the past six
years in Holister, Massachusetts. Integrated advertising and local cultural information into a yearly program book, from which all profits are contributed to a
local charity.

Advertising Editor for the Holister State University newspaper:
1988 - 1990

SEMINARS & WORKSHOPS
Dale Carnegie course in Public Speaking
Newton, Massachusetts 1992

Creative Writing
Newton, Massachusetts 1993

REFERENCES
Available upon request.

CANDACE L. MINOT

2343 Robin Lane • Santee, CA 91076
619/555-1224 • Candy_Minot@xxx.com

Objective

A position as an office manager in the health field.

Achievements

- Implemented a program that increased work efficiency among nonmanagement employees.
- Inaugurated a leadership program that increased productivity by 20 percent among non-management employees.
- Developed a billing system that cut accounting procedures by 50 percent.

Work Experience

La Jolla Dental Group, La Jolla, CA
Office Manager, 1984 - 1986
Managed an office of five employees whose duties included billing, ordering supplies, reception, and acted as liaisons to the insurance companies and the dentists.

Pacific Gas and Electric Co., Redlands, CA
Accounts Receivable Clerk, 1980 - 1984
Maintained billing and collection records. Also, provided customer service to customers with billing disputes.

Redwood City Water Department, Redwood City, CA
Receptionist, 1978 - 1980
Duties: Greeted customers and made appointments for meter inspectors.

Workshops & Seminars

Course in Herbology:
The importance of herbs in medical treatments, instructed by Claire Caldwell: May 2001

Raw Foods Seminar:
Healing properties of raw foods instructed by Dr. Ann Wigmore of Hippocrates Institute: July 2001

Education

San Diego Business School, San Diego, CA
Major: Office Management; Certificate: 1977

References

Provided on request.

ELAINE REYNOLDS

2324 Wainwright Drive
Marionville, NJ 08229
609/555-8965

CAREER OBJECTIVE
A position as a TV sales host for a cable television shopping network.

EXPERIENCE
WKBC Cable Entertainment Network, Philadelphia, PA
Advertising Sales Representative, 1996 - 1999
Sold TV advertising spots within six counties to merchants, businesses, and services. Consistently achieved annual sales goal quota of $300,000.

Cherry Hill Herald Daily News, **Cherry Hill, NJ**
Sales Representative, 1992 - 1996
Processed classified advertising sales orders over the telephone and conducted direct sales calls.

Bergen Bulletin Weekly, **Bergen, NJ**
Receptionist/Clerk, 1990 - 1992
Greeted clients, transferred incoming calls, managed all correspondence, and created ad copy.

EDUCATION
Philadelphia School of Visual Arts, Philadelphia, PA
Major: TV and Radio Broadcasting and Advertising
Diploma awarded 1989

RELATED ACTIVITIES
- WKBC TV sales host fill-in for the New Product Department segment when regular hosts were on vacation.

- Assistant TV sales auctioneer for annual children's summer camp benefit program sponsored by WKBC.

HONORS
- Recipient of the Philadelphia School of Visual Arts annual award for the most accomplished student in the School of Broadcasting, 1989.

- Dean's List, five semesters.

REFERENCES
Furnished upon request.

REBECCA BOSANGE

12 Delaney St. • Revere, MA 06125 • 617/555-8975
beckybosange@xxx.com

OBJECTIVE
To obtain the position of a nanny in a private residence.

EXPERIENCE
Nanny, Somerset, Bermuda, 1993 - 1998
Cared for two children from the ages of 18 months and 2 months in a private residence, for five years. Duties included monitoring their playtime activities, teaching them the French language, supervising dietary menus, and encouraging healthy outdoor activities with children of their own age.

Language Instructor, Marseilles, France, 1998 - 2000
Taught 3 children in one family ages 2, 3, and 5 years old the English language.

EDUCATION
Boston College, Newton, MA, 1990 - 1994
Major: Child Psychology
Graduated *summa cum laude*

Marseilles School of Cooking, Marseilles, France
Course of studies included canapes, entrees, and desserts.
Certificate awarded, 1996.

RELATED ACTIVITIES
Organized a program of outdoor summer activities for children ages 10 - 17 years old, at the Brookville Housing Development, Brookville, MA, 1992 - 1994.

Coordinated an annual Christmas party for young children at the Brookville Housing Development, Brookville, MA, 1991 - 1993.

ACHIEVEMENT
Coauthored *The Children's Book of Games*, published by Playtime Publishers of London, 1995.

HOBBIES
Writing, cooking, travel.

REFERENCES
Furnished upon request.

ANTOINETTE B. STEVENS

• 1080 Collette Lane • Tulsa, Oklahoma • 77402 • Cellular: 405/555-3060 •

OBJECTIVE
To obtain a position as a manager/supervisor for a retail grocery corporation.

EXPERIENCE
Pears, Plums and Pomegranates, Specialty Fruit Basket Shop/Tulsa
President and owner, 1990 - 1995
Founded and owned a specialty fresh fruit basket shop where customers could select various fruit for individually created gift baskets. Handled sales internally and on phone/fax. Managed three employees, conducted all purchasing, inventory control, payroll, and bookkeeping. Store sold in 1995.

Kroger Food Emporium, Inc./Tulsa
Purchasing Coordinator, 1987 - 1990
Responsibilities included development and implementation of computerized purchasing. Developed and instructed training of personnel in Direct Vendor Contract purchasing, operations, procedures, and inventory.

Fisher Fine Foods, Inc./Oklahoma City
Personnel/Payroll Administrator, 1983 - 1987
Responsible for payroll, insurance, and personnel screening for three regional stores. Duties included: indoctrination of new employees, claims processing, maintenance and payment of group medical/dental insurance. Reported monthly and quarterly payroll tax, and Workers' Compensation. Worked with ADP field services in solving programming problems as well as new hardware implementations.

Barker Regional Food Wholesalers, Inc./Oklahoma City
Accounting/Treasury Liaison, 1977 - 1983
Duties involved accounts payable and receivable, payroll, and analysis of ledger accounts. Served as liaison for accounting and treasury, handling all facets of banking for treasury and expense accounting. Assisted in the development and utilization of a new payroll system.

EDUCATION
University of Oklahoma/Tulsa
B.S. in Business, Degree awarded in 1977
Major: Marketing; Minor: Accounting

Midwest City College/Midwest City
Personnel Development: Design of Training Programs, 1983

CTI, Computer Training Institute/Oklahoma City
World Wide Web resources; Lotus; and MS Office including Word, PowerPoint, and Excel

REFERENCES
Furnished upon request.

ELIZABETH R. CAMPBELL
622 Byrn Avenue
Houston, TX 77504
Cellular Phone: 713/555-7878
lizcampbell@xxx.com

OBJECTIVE
A position as a job recruiter in a personnel office or agency where my experience can be utilized.

EDUCATION
Kent State University/Kent, OH, 1974 - 1978
B.S. in Human Resources; Dean's List 1978

PROFESSIONAL EXPERIENCE
Jobcorp Employment Agency/Pittsburgh, PA
Placement Officer: 1983 - 1990
Interviewed candidates for full- and part-time employment opportunities. Conducted testing in clerical and aptitude requirements designated by employer. Interviewed college seniors on local college campuses.

Snelling and Snelling Agency, Inc./Kent, OH
Receptionist/Secretary: 1979 - 1983
Coordinated appointments for clients. Typed correspondence and maintained filing system. Periodically interviewed clients for part-time manual labor positions.

SUMMARY OF QUALIFICATIONS
- Project oriented and motivated to complete challenging tasks.
- Work well under stressful conditions.
- Conduct and maintain well-organized interviews.

MEMBERSHIPS
- Toastmasters Organization, 1999 - present
  Office held: Recording Secretary, 2001
- Sigma, Sigma, Sigma Social Sorority, Active: 1975 - 1978
  Office held: Vice President, 1977

HONORS
- Toastmaster of the Year Award, 2001
- Article entitled "Getting That First Job," published in the *Job Market* magazine, April 1989

REFERENCES
Available upon request.

Stanislaw Yershonak

13410 15th Street • Flushing, New York 12139
(718) 555-1734 • yershonak@xxx.com

Career Objective

To utilize my previous medical training in dentistry and apply for a residency in Oral and Maxillofacial Surgery.

Education

Riga Medical Institute, Riga, Latvia
Curriculum: General Medicine
Physician of Stomatology Degree awarded in 1997

New York University, College of Dentistry, New York, NY
Degree in Dentistry awarded in 2001

Work History

Montefiore Medical Center, New York, NY
GP Residency, 2001 - 2002

Central Latvian Republic Heart and Vessel Surgery Clinic
Physicians Assistant, 1992 - 1993
Worked in the resuscitation and Intensive Care Department

Yurmala City Hospital, Yurmala, Latvia
Nurses Assistant and EMT, part-time, 1989 - 1991
Worked in the Cardiopulmonary Resuscitation Ambulance Unit Department

Honors & Awards

New York University College of Dentistry, 2002
"The Division of Comprehensive Care, Applied Practice Administration and Behavioral Sciences, Bernard E. Rudner Memorial Award," for superior performance in providing oral comprehensive care in managing a dental practice.

Central Latvian Republic Heart and Vessel Surgery Clinic
Conducted research that was presented at the Third Congress of Baltic States Cardiologists and was published in *Prophylaxis, Diagnostics and Treatments of Cardiovascular Disease*, and in the textbook of the 35th Medical Scientific Conference, Riga, Latvia, 1995

Volunteer

Dedicated a year of dental practice to the Medical and Dental
Clinic in Riga, Latvia, to assist the young and the elderly in need of dental care, 2000.

Memberships

- National Society of Dentistry, New York Chapter
- Latvian Foreign Student Exchange Program; office held: President, 2000.
- Latvian Cultural Affairs Organization, New York

References

Furnished upon request.

Ramon C. Cortez
3856 N. Harvard Avenue • Washington, D.C. 20023 • Home: 202/555-3355

Career Objective

To become a Medical Transcriptionist and utilize my past medical experience as a foundation.

Summary of Qualifications

- Self-starter and perfectionist
- Self-disciplined and committed to learning
- Strong interest in medicine
- Able to concentrate for long periods
- Willing to assist others
- Able to work with minimal supervision
- Dedicated to professional development and achievement.

Education

Bethesda Medical Training Institute, Bethesda, Maryland
Medical Transcriptionist: Two-year program; Diploma, 1997
Curriculum included the following courses: Stenotype, Medical/Legal Dictation, Word Processing, Medical Terminology, Anatomy and Physiology, Pharmacology, Human Diseases and Surgical Problems.

Capitol Community College, Washington, D.C.
Administrative Technical Training: Certification, 1995
Course study and application of computer training in the following programs: Lotus, Microsoft Word, Excel, and Access.

Employment

Wolfert Pharmaceutical Supply, Washington, D.C.
Supply Clerk, part-time, 1994 - 2000
Filled orders and packed pharmaceutical supplies for shipping to medical offices and facilities.

Drug Castle Chemists, Washington, D.C.
Sales Clerk, 1989 - 1994
Conducted cash and credit card sales transactions. Stocked merchandise, delivered prescription drugs, assisted in training new personnel.

References

Available upon request.

Marlene Rief

223 South Bentley   (313) 555-7894
Marionville, MI 48231   mreif@xxx.com

CAREER OBJECTIVE: To utilize my experience as a flight attendant for an
                          international air carrier.

WORK EXPERIENCE: **Pan American World Airways, New York, NY**
                          Flight Attendant, 1983 - 1990
                          Responsible for the safety of passengers during a flight. Served
                          beverages and meals, monitored unaccompanied minor chil-
                          dren, assisted passengers with small children and elderly
                          passengers traveling with medical restrictions.

                          Travel World, Inc., Marionville, MI
                          Travel Consultant, 1991 - 1997
                          Booked travel arrangements, hotel accommodations, and auto-
                          mobile reservations for clients. Planned ground tours worldwide.
                          Conducted tours in Europe and North America as a tour guide.
                          Coordinated cruise line vacations and African safari expeditions.

EDUCATION: Pan American Flight Attendant Training School
                          New York, NY -- 1983
                          Training included emergency procedure course in aircraft
                          evacuation, first aid, and CPR. The serving of food and bever-
                          ages. Positive communication while under stress. Courses in
                          grooming, health, and exercise.

                          Michigan State University, Dearborn campus, Dearborn, MI
                          Bachelor of Science in Education, Degree, 1983
                          Homecoming Queen, 1982 football season

SKILLS: • Fluent in English, French, and Spanish
                          • Working knowledge of the Apollo and Sable airline computer
                            systems

REFERENCES: Available upon request.

CAROL SCHMIDT

12 Overlook Drive
Denver, Colorado 88021
Pager: (303) 555-4467
cschmidt@xxx.com

OBJECTIVE

To seek a position as a travel consultant within a travel facility with opportunities for advancement.

PROFESSIONAL EXPERIENCE

Lufthansa German Airlines
Los Angeles, California
Reservation Sales, 1995 - 1999
Provided travel arrangement reservations for passengers. Computed international fares and taxes; secured hotel and car reservations; arranged sale of ticket with credit card, travel agency, or airline ticket office. Working knowledge of the Siemans and Amadeus computer program system. Training course successfully completed in Germany: Advanced Reservations, Psychology in Sales, and Quality in Daily Work.

South African Airways
San Francisco, California
Customer Service Reservation Sales, 1992 - 1995
Booked international reservations using the Safari computer program system, with passengers, tour operators, wholesale consolidators, and travel agents. Courses successfully completed: Effective Sales Techniques in Reservations, Johannesburg, South Africa. International Fare Calculation, New York City.

Premier Travel Agency
Denver, Colorado
Travel Agent, 1989 - 1992
Booked vacation and corporate travel reservations for clients on the phone and in person including hotel, car, cruise ship, and rail reservations.

EDUCATION

Atlantic Travel Agents School, Kansas City, Kansas
Certification, 1989
Comprehensive training in all phases of air, land, and sea reservation-booking transactions. Manual and computer fare calculation, ticket issue, agency accounting systems, and general office duties.

SUMMARY OF QUALIFICATIONS

- Ability to work well under pressure and to get the job done sucessfully.
- Well-traveled and knowledgeable of the mores and customs of various cultures.
- Able to work on a variety of projects simultaneously to successful completion of tasks.
- Proficient in five airline computer systems.

HONORS & AWARDS

- Top sales revenue agent at Lufthansa, Los Angeles, 2001.
- Highest score in Fare Calculation course, New York City, 1994
- Travel Agent of the Year Award, Denver, 1991.

REFERENCES

Furnished upon request

ROLANDA MARIE PAGANINI

3212 Loganberry Avenue
Cedar Rapids, Iowa 52447
319/555-8877
Paganini@xxx.com

OBJECTIVE

A challenging position as a graphic artist in which my computer and educational background can be utilized.

QUALIFICATIONS

- Highly motivated and dependable in achieving goals.
- Strong organizational skills, attention to detail.
- Ability to analyze and solve problems in a constantly changing work environment.
- Self-motivated and confident in making independent decisions.
- Competitive, efficient, hard working, and enthusiastic.

EDUCATION

Cedar Rapids School of Visual Arts, Cedar Rapids, Iowa
A.S. Degree in Graphic Design, 1995

CTC Computer Training College, Cedar Rapids, Iowa
Certificate received, 1993
Curriculum: PC training including computerized Accounting and Microsoft Suite including Word, PowerPoint, Access, and Excel

EMPLOYMENT

NATIONWIDE COMPUTER OUTLET STORE, IOWA CITY, IOWA
ADVERTISING DEPARTMENT, 1996 - 2000
Assisted Art Director in creating graphic art for weekly newspaper advertising. Researched competitive ads in the central Midwest and maintained files in order to prevent duplication.

ABC ARTS, INC., CEDAR RAPIDS, IOWA
ASSISTANT MANAGER, 1993 - 1996
Responsible for three part-time employees, trained new personnel, ordered stock for two stores, evaluated employee performance.

INTERESTS

Oil painting, photography, stained-glass art.

REFERENCES

Furnished upon request.

REGINALD D. DAWSON

4800 Johnson Plank Road • Albuquerque, NM 87819
505-555-4889 • r_dawson@xxx.com

JOB OBJECTIVE

To seek a position as a physical therapist assistant while continuing my studies in physical therapy.

EDUCATION

University of New Mexico/Albuquerque Campus
Physical Therapy curriculum; completed 2 years, received certification for Physical Therapy Assistant - 1995.
Continuing program in evening division commencing September, 1999. Projected graduation date with a B.S. in Physical Therapy, December 2002.

Santa Fe School of Massage/Santa Fe
Certified in 1990. Course consisted of the study and application of Shiatsu and Swedish massage, hand and foot reflexology, therapeutic mineral massage, and deep heat massage.

Acupuncture School of New Mexico/Santa Fe
Certified in 1990. Studied Acupuncture application for remedy of headaches, bronchial conditions, bursitis, arthritis, tendinitis, and lower back ailments.

WORK EXPERIENCE

CITY OF ALBUQUERQUE, Department of Social Services
Paramedic, 1985 - 1990

U.S. NAVY, Basic Training/Great Lakes, IL
Hospital Corpsman, 1982 - 1985
Trained for rating of Hospital Corpsman in San Diego. Tour of duty served in Panama and Kuwait.

SEMINARS

- Rolfing, March 1992
- Healing properties of Raw Foods, Viktoras Kulvanskas, September 1992
- Goal Setting, Anthony Robbins, 1993

AWARDS & MEMBERSHIPS

- Dean's List, 1993 - 1994
- U.S. Paramedics Association
- Second-highest grade average, Hospital Corpsman School

REFERENCES

Available on request.

Horoko Kimura

111 Southwest Blvd.
East Providence, RI 02777
401/555-4871
Kimura@xxx.com

CAREER OBJECTIVE

Seeking a staff accountant position enabling me to utilize my diverse skills, knowledge, and experience, that simultaneously offers an opportunity for growth and advancement.

SKILLS & ACHIEVEMENTS

- Designed a user friendly Lotus template for project development staff providing an instrument of measurement to track investment contract expenditures.
- Streamlined time spent processing payroll and improved accuracy by implementing automated time clock system to replace punch clock format.
- Improved efficiency and growth of project direction by taking an active role in communicating daily with the departments involved in investment contracts.

EMPLOYMENT HISTORY

Rankin, Smith and Hightower Investment Group, Inc. - Providence, RI
Senior Staff Accountant, 1993 - 2000
Prepared and reviewed financial statements for management, assisted in annual budgeting, audited disbursements for accuracy and validity, and maintained commission programs.

Margate & Paynter Financial Brokers, Inc. - Providence, RI
Accounting Clerk, 1990 - 1993
Prepared weekly physical inventory report and reconciliation, monthly accounts receivable aging report, sales and purchase ledger reconciliation, invoice coding, and product sales pricing. Developed and installed new coding program, assisted in reprogramming of invoice and collection data system.

EDUCATION

University of Providence - Providence, RI
B.S. in Accounting, GPA 3.6
Degree awarded: 2001
A.S. in Accounting, GPA 3.4
Associate degree awarded: 1992

SUMMARY OF QUALIFICATIONS

- Eagerly accept challenges and new opportunities.
- Strong analytical and problem-solving abilities.
- Project and goal oriented.
- Easily adapt to new systems and programs.

COMPUTER SKILLS

Microsoft Applications including: Word, Excel, PowerPoint, and Publisher.
Lotus 1-2-3, Professional Write, and PageMaker.

REFERENCES

Furnished upon request.

BRIAN P. MILLER

212 Brookside Avenue East • Portland, Oregon 97786
503/555-2238 • bmiller@xxx.com

OBJECTIVE

A responsible and challenging managerial position where my extensive supervisory background can be utilized to achieve company goals.

EDUCATION

University of Oregon - Portland, Oregon; MBA in Business Management, 1983 Honors: Dean's List, 1981 - 1983

Hooper-Paterson College, Eugene, Oregon; B.S. in Marketing, 1981
Honors: Dean's List, 1978 - 1981

PROFESSIONAL EXPERIENCE

Operations Manager, Euro Auto Car Leasing Company
London, England, 1990 - 1999
Responsible for the largest region in the country, with a $2.5 million USD per month revenue and 250 fleet accounts. Servicing all lease customers with respect to purchasing new vehicles and facilitating delivery. Implemented preventive maintenance program, established a dealer network for cost effective purchasing of new vehicles. Supervised a staff of twelve maintenance and purchasing coordinators. Conducted program planning and presentation, projected account profitability, maintained profitability reports and analyses.

Account Manager, Dictaphone Corporation
Salem, Oregon, 1983 - 1990
Established service agreement accounts, prospected for leads and referrals, maintained branch inventory on all stock. Monitored activity and technological advancements of competitors and emphasized similar features in sales presentations.

AWARDS

• Manager of the Year, European Division, Euro Auto Car Leasing, 1994 and 1999.
• Best Performance New Sales Representative, Dictaphone Corporation, 1983.

SUMMARY OF ACHIEVEMENTS

- Developed training programs that have enhanced sales performance and directly increased sales revenue by 15 percent.
- Have decreased maintenance expenses 20 percent by implementing preventive check-ups at each delivery port-of-call transfer.
- Established an incentive program for station managers that rewarded outstanding employee achievements and recognized employee efforts for positive public relations.
- Initiated a monthly news report to keep all stations abreast of company administration, personnel, and internal affairs information and changes.

REFERENCES

Furnished upon request.

MICHAEL C. COOPER

87 Sherwood Court
Joliet, IL 34122
312/555-0967
mike_cooper@xxx.com

OBJECTIVE

Seeking a position as a director of a nonprofit organization with the primary role of a fund raiser.

SUMMARY OF ACHIEVEMENTS

- Organized a a chapel fund drive for St. Francis' Children's Summer Camp. Donations in excess of $500,000.

- Coordinated a trust fund drive for the Senior Citizens' Retirement Home in Joliet. Contributions totaled $350,000.

- Planned week-long event for Papal visit during summer of 1993. Organized hotel accommodations for visiting dignitaries and scheduled the daily seminars and guest speakers' agendas.

EDUCATION

University of Notre Dame, South Bend, IN
M.D. in Theology, 1977
Curriculum included: Communications and Counseling, Scripture, Ecclesiology, History
Newman College, Baltimore, MD
B.A. in History, 1972

PROFESSIONAL EXPERIENCE

St. Francis Catholic Church, Joliet, IL
Pastor 1980 - 1994

Xavier High School for Boys, Chicago, IL
Instructor, Department of History, 1978 - 1980
Coach, Junior Varsity Baseball Team

ARTICLES PUBLISHED

"The Role of Religion in Today's High-Tech Environment"
"Integrating Religion in the Sports Arena"

SUMMARY OF QUALIFICATIONS

Well-rounded education.
Ability to communicate to large groups of people.
Trained to lead from consensus.

REFERENCES

Furnished upon request.

SUZANNE M. GEORGE

7919 Ragland Drive
Girard, OH 44484
Pager: 216/555-5647

Objective

To obtain a position in the field of news reporting.

Education

Youngstown State University, Youngstown, OH, 1990 - 1994
BS in Journalism with a 3.9 G.P.A.

Experience

Niles Daily Times, Niles, OH, 1997 - 1999
News Desk Reporter/Clerk: Duties included proofreading articles
submitted by local reporters. Wrote local society column including
various area events. Compiled feature articles on celebrities appearing at the Kenley Players summer stock theater in Warren, OH.

WKBN Television/Radio Station, Youngstown, OH, 1994 - 1997
Junior Reporter: Assisted news team with media coverage on trips throughout the local viewing area in the WKBN Action Van. Wrote reviews of local college and high school plays for WKBN radio. Responsible for updating media files.

Related Experience

- Wrote human interest articles that were published in local newspapers including topics such as child guidance, destruction of the rain forest, global warming, and the effects of stress in today's competitive job market.
- Developed a weekly column for the Youngstown University newspaper capping all the social and charitable events sponsored by all the fraternities and sororities on campus.
- Hosted a monthly FM radio program on WYSU, a university-sponsored radio station, interviewing professors teaching in the various schools at the university.
- Tutor foreign residents in ESL classes at Howland High School in Warren.

Hobbies

Writing short stories and poetry; reading.

References

Furnished upon request.

• *Roger G. Caisser*

125 Morley Drive
Little Rock, Arkansas 84542
Home: 501/555-1232
Cell: 501/555-1214

Career Objective

To obtain a managerial position whereby my past business experience and raising of six children have given me the tools to be effectively diplomatic and enterprising.

Management Achievements

- Structured setting of goals to achieve the desired best for the majority involved.
- Developed routines that are varied enough to keep interest and incentive at a high level.
- Revised game plan so that all employees are kept aware of importance of colleagues' relationships to one another.
- Improved upper management relationship with nonmanagement with monthly review and action on employee concerns.
- Inaugurated motivational seminars for all employees for personal development that is beneficial to their business and private lives.
- Established a monthly newsletter that featured several employees and their contributions to the success of the organization.

Work Experience

Aaron Public Gas and Electric Co., Little Rock, Arkansas
Manager, Residential Division, 1987 - 1993
Supervised 80 employees ranging from entry-level clerical to middle management.

Little Rock Water Department, Little Rock, Arkansas
Supervisor, Meter Maintenance Division, 1982 - 1987
Water Meter Installation Engineer, 1980 - 1982

City Hall, City of Little Rock, Arkansas
Administrative Clerk, City Tax Department, 1976 - 1980
Maintained residential tax billing files, sent out biyearly property tax invoices, conducted audits, and assisted with monthly inventory assessment files.

Military

U.S. Marines, United States of America
Captain, 1973 - 1976
Served in both Viet Nam and Panama.

Education

University of Little Rock, Little Rock, Arkansas
School of Business
Major: Accounting; Minor: Economics
Degree awarded 1972

Volunteer Activities

- Little League baseball coach.
- Sunday school teacher for elementary grade students.
- Junior Achievement sponsor.
- Swimming instructor at children's summer camp.
- Coordinator for Senior High School annual trip to Washington, D.C.

References

Available upon request.

SHANIQUA THOMAS

5622 Hedgwick Road • Charlestown, NH 03976
Home: 603/555-2489 • Pager: 603/555-3114

OBJECTIVE

Seeking a challenging and responsible patrolman's position where law enforcement knowledge and skill can be extensively utilized with opportunities for growth and advancement.

EDUCATION

MTC Training Center/Concord, NH
New Hampshire Basic Police Academy
New Hampshire State Certification, 1997 - 1999

Masters Training Systems /Concord, NH
Basic Certification, August 1999
• Surveillance Techniques

Law Enforcement Training Systems Institute/Manchester, NH
Achieved certification in the following categories in May 1999:
• Use of Force Liability and Subject Control
• Strategies and Tactics of Patrol Stops

Law Enforcement Training Systems Institute/Concord, NH
Achieved certification in the following categories in March 1999:
• Courtroom Testimony
• Rules of Evidence
• New Hampshire DUI Laws/Legal Update
• Horizontal Gaze and Nystagmus /DUI Detection

Management Systems, Inc. /Manchester, NH
Basic Certification, June 1995
• Pressure Point Control Tactics Defensive Systems

EMPLOYMENT

Pinkerton's Security Systems, Inc./Claremont, NH
Sales Representative, 1990 - 1995
Demonstrated security systems to customers for home and commercial use in showroom. Tested new systems after installation and instructed clients in operation of system.

REFERENCES

Furnished upon request.

Lisa Homedes

2870 Cross Line Road
Orangeburg, NY 14398
(914) 555-3740

Objective

To obtain a position as a sous chef.

Education

The Culinary School of Arts /Poughkeepsie, NY
Course of study included the preparation of appetizers, entrees, and desserts. Cooked foods of different cultures, mainly French, Italian, and Spanish. Educated on wine selections from around the world. Instruction on table settings for every occasion. Interpretation of recipes for increasing or decreasing ingredients proportionate to the quantity desired.
Diploma, 1999

Sparkill College/Sparkill, NY
A.S. in Business; Major: Accounting
Degree, 1990

Experience

The Gun Powder Cavern/Pomona, NY -- Internship, Summer 1999
Assisted chef in preparation of lunch and dinner menus. Responsibilities included keeping kitchen utensils in organizational readiness, all spices and herbs at near capacity level, and all menus updated to reflect the specials of the day.

Western Auto Hardware Store/Tappan, NY -- Bookkeeper, 1990 - 1994
Duties included accounts receivable and payable, assisting in payroll calculation, and maintaining files for payroll.

Palisades Diner/Tappan, NY -- Waitress, 1985 - 1990
Served lunch and dinner entrees.

Honors & Awards

Graduated top 5 percent of class, The Culinary School of Arts.
Dean's List, Sparkill College, 1988 - 1990

Memberships

Future Chefs of America (FCA), Poughkeepsie Chapter. Recording Secretary, 1998
National Accounting Fraternity, Sparkill College

References

Available upon request

JILL REISMAN

●●●

80 Crescent Circle
Hinsdale, IL 60870
j_reisman@xxx.com
708/555-2568

●●● OBJECTIVE

To obtain a position as a hostess/party counselor for a restaurant or party center.

●●● SUMMARY OF QUALIFICATIONS

- Organizational and problem-solving capabilities.
- Excellent motivational skills.
- Eager to accept challenging tasks.
- Ready to assist where help is needed.
- Outstanding work performance.
- Congenial professional attitude.

●●● RELATED ACTIVITIES

- Organized and coordinated banquet dinner parties, dinner dances, class reunions, holiday event parties, and wedding receptions.
- Assisted in planning daily menus for elementary schools, convalescent homes, and day care centers.
- Consultant to various companies and businesses planning awards and retirement functions.

●●● EMPLOYMENT

The Cranston Country Club/Hinsdale, IL
Hostess and Manager, 1996 - 2000
Managed main dining room and coffee bar. Seated customers, supervised eight waiters and four lunch counter personnel. Responsible for all table and counter set-ups. Hired and trained staff, planned work schedules, and took table reservations.

The Biltmore Hotel/Chicago, IL
Dining Room Hostess, 1992 - 1995
Seated dinner guests. Filled in as assistant dining room manager during assistant manager's vacation. Recorded hotel guests' dinner charges for front desk accounting records. Conducted biyearly inventory of table linens, dinnerware, and silverware. Assisted in recruitment of personnel.

Page 1 of 2

••• EDUCATION

University of Illinois/Chicago, IL
Major: Bachelor of Fine Arts; Degree, 1991
Awards: *Cum laude,* Dean's List, 1990 - 1991

Memberships: Beta Sigma Omicron Social Sorority; offices held:
Recording Secretary, 1983 - 1984,
Vice President, 1984 - 1985
Students for the Appreciation of Fine Arts Association, 1982 - 1985

••• SEMINARS

- Hotel Dining Room Management, Carbondale, IL -- June 1993.
- Dining Table Art, Chicago School of Design, Chicago, IL -- September 1994.
- European Hotel Cuisine, International Cooking School, Chicago, IL -- November 1994.
- Wines Worldwide, Midwest Wine Conference, Chicago, IL -- October 1995.
- Introduction to Computerized Inventories for Food Services, New York, NY -- May 1996.

••• REFERENCES

Available upon request.

ROBERTA G. SMITH
3478 Anderson Avenue
Clarenceville, NY 11754
716/555-4322

OBJECTIVE
To obtain a position as a Veterinary Technician

EDUCATION
Farmingdale College of Veterinary Medicine/Farmingdale, NY
A.S. Veterinary Technician, 1997

Wendell's School of Animal Behavior/Beth Page, NY
Dog Obedience Certification: 1996

Hofstra University/Hofstra, NY
A.S. Business Management, 1990

EMPLOYMENT
Pet Nosh Pet Supplies/Valley Stream, NY, 1991 - 1997
Manager: Supervised three employees, planned monthly work schedules, ordered stock weekly. Responsible for all newspaper and TV/radio advertising. Coordinated yearly Christmas card picture of customers' pets photographed with Santa that increased sales during December by 40 percent.

Campus Kennels/Westbury, NY, 1989 - 1991
Canine Maintenance Technician: Responsible for all aspects of the care of animals boarded at the kennel. Fed them daily, took them on walks and on runs, kept their living areas clean and supplied with fresh water, gave them care and attention to make them feel comfortable while away from home.

RELATED ACTIVITIES
- Volunteer at the North Shore Animal Shelter/Syosset, NY, 1991 - 1997.
- Breed Dalmatians and have shown at AKC-sponsored contests and events.

HONORS
- Received the "Most Dedicated Student" award during last semester attending Farmingdale College.
- Awarded "Volunteer of the Year" citation from the North Shore Animal League, 1997.

REFERENCES
Available upon request.

J O H N   P .   R O D G E R S
3478 Harmon Cove Rd.
Lincoln, NE 68990
402/555-9956
JPRodgers@xxx.com

OBJECTIVE: To obtain a position as an administrative assistant.

EXPERIENCE: U.S. Naval Facility, San Juan, PR, 1992 - 1994
Captain's Yeoman, Administrative assistant to the Captain of the Naval Facility. Answered the phone; typed correspondence and military directives; assisted Captain during monthly Naval personnel inspections.

U.S. Naval Communications Station, Iceland, 1990 - 1992
Commander's Yeoman, Administrative assistant to the Commander of the Communication Station. Answered the phone; processed personnel on orders to the command; organized and maintained active roster for the Ground Defense Force, Iceland.

PART-TIME EMPLOYMENT: Food waiter, Officer's Club - Keflavik, Iceland
Assistant Librarian, San Juan, PR

EDUCATION: Canton Community College - Canton, NE
A.S. in Business Management, 1988
G.P.A. 3.6

Communications Yeoman School, Norfolk, VA
Appointed Company Officer for the 3-month course
Awarded certification November 1989.

SUMMARY OF QUALIFICATIONS:
- Enthusiastic with a can-do attitude.
- Experienced in conducting training seminars detailing office procedures and practices.
- Strong interpersonal and communication skills.
- Successful goal-achievement record and team player.

AWARDS:
- Yeoman of the Month - Keflavik, Iceland, May 1990
- Highest Score Award certificate, Communications
- Yeoman School, Norfolk, VA, November 1989

REFERENCES: Available upon request.

DELORES A. GRIFFITH

3215 HIGHLAND AVE.
MANHATTAN, KS 66500
CELL: 316-555-6767

OBJECTIVE
Seeking a position as a sales representative within the retail industry.

EDUCATION
Manhattan Community College, Manhattan, KS
A.S. in Business Administration - 1987
Major: Retail Merchandising; GPA: 3.7

Williamson High School
Williamson, KS; Diploma - 1985
Senior Class President
Student Council Vice President

EMPLOYMENT
<u>Kaufman's Department Store, Kansas City, KS</u>
Retail Sales Clerk, Women's Apparel Department
Top 10 percent of retail clerks in revenue sales, 1996 - 1999.

<u>Sallie's Gift and Boutique Shop, Manhattan, KS</u>
Sales Clerk - Responsible for opening the shop each day and performed all sales
transactions, 1991 - 1996.

<u>Rite-Aid Drug Store, Manhattan, KS</u>
Sales/Stock Clerk - Stocked shelves with merchandise, assisted with inventory
control, made sales transactions, delivered prescriptions for pharmacy, 1987 - 1991.

PART-TIME EMPLOYMENT
<u>Avon Company, New York, NY</u>
Sales Representative/Team Leader, Eastern Kansas
Have been successful sales/team leader since 1995 and have maintained a sales
staff of approximately 30 part-time team members. Sales revenue for this division
has consistently been in the top 10 percent of total sales revenue estimated annually
for central Midwest localities.

ACTIVITIES
- Coordinated Chinese Auction Charity Bazaar for the Senior Citizen Community
  Center of Manhattan, KS.
- Organized the annual "Toys for Tots" campaign with donations from local
  merchants during holiday season in Manhattan, KS, since 2000.

REFERENCES
Furnished upon request.

Maryellen Grace

8693 Elan Drive • Boca Raton, FL 33058
Cellular: 407-555-2324 • E-mail: mgrace@xxx.com

• *Objective*
To utilize my showroom and administrative skills within the fashion industry.

• *Education*
French Fashion Academy, New York, NY
Diploma granted: 1984
Studies included pattern designing, pattern grading, and constructing clothes from commercial and self-designed patterns. Received French Fashion Academy award for designing the most innovative/functional women's all-weather evening coat in case study for final exam.

Wilfred Academy of Beauty, New York, NY
Certificate awarded 1984
Program course was based on the skillful application of makeup for daytime, evening, high-fashion, and theatrical purposes. Awarded first place in class competition for high-fashion makeup application.

Miami Business College, Miami, FL
Diploma granted, 1981
Course studies included secretarial skills with intensive training on computer applications in bookkeeping, filing, and correspondence.

• *Employment*
Lily Rubin Designers, Inc., Fort Lauderdale, FL
Design Assistant/Showroom Reception: 1984 - 1994
Assist designers in applying makeup to models wearing their creations. Assembled and distributed press kits to buyers and fashion editors.

Theodore Green and Sons, Diamond Co., New York, NY
Secretary/Receptionist: Part-time employment, 1981 - 1984
Duties: Typed correspondence, answered phone, greeted buyers, set appointments, assisted clientele in jewelry selections. Assisted in representing company during annual jewelry show held in a different major city each year.

• *Related Activities*
- Implemented a workshop for the busy working woman in applying makeup using shortcuts that give the same results in half the time. Have conducted this seminar at numerous companies and business offices in the south Florida area since 2000.
- Developed and organized a fashion show for the Merchants' Association of the Fort Lauderdale Southern Park Mall during the Christmas holidays, 2001.
- Guest speaker on high-fashion clothes and makeup at local high schools throughout the year.

• *Organizations*
- President of PTA, Goodwin Marshall Elementary School, 1998 - 2000.
- Recording Secretary, Fort Lauderdale Historical Society, 2001.

• *References*
Available upon request.

NATASHA L. WOODBINE
21101 Locust Valley Rd.
Marlburg, TN 37223
615/555-3684

Job Objective
A position that will best utilize my secretarial experience.

Professional Experience
U.S. Naval Station, Rhodes, Greece
Secretary to the Commander, 1990 - 1993
Organized meeting places for the Commander when visiting dignitaries were invited to conferences under the NATO agreement. Typed and sent United States confidential and secret messages to various command centers throughout the world. Maintained confidential and secret files. Arranged government transportation requests for officers and enlisted personnel and their families.

Moreland Savings and Loan Banking Company, Moreland, TN
Secretary to the Loan Officer, 1987 - 1990
Typed loan applications, posted all lease payments, and quoted buyout figures.

Education
Waverly Secretarial School, Knoxville, TN
A.S. in Office Procedures, 1986
Courses included: Typing; Dictation; Computer Training Skills in Windows, Lotus 1-2-3, Word Processing, and Graphics.

Awards & Honors
- Valedictorian of the graduation class, Waverly Secretarial School, 1986
- Secretary of the month, June 1992, U.S. Naval Communication Station, Rhodes, Greece.

Special Qualifications
Secret and Confidential clearance status issued by the United States Government.

References
Available upon request.

Pushpa Patel

1744 Winding Oak Lane • Dallas, Texas 73499
Cellular: 214-555-8001 • P_Patel@xxx.com

Career Objective

To obtain a position as a Pharmacy Technician while pursuing my educational studies to obtain a degree in Pharmacology.

Education

University of Dallas, Dallas, Texas
B.S. in Pharmaceutical Procedures
Diploma, 2000

University of Bombay, Bombay, India
Major: Hospital Administration
Total credits earned: 64, 1986

Employment

CVS Drug Store, Irving, Texas
Sales Clerk, part-time, 1995 - 1998
Conducted sales transactions and assisted customers in merchandise selections.

VA Hospital, Fort Worth, Texas
Administrative Assistant, 1992 - 1995
Directed internal calls, maintained record file system, set appointments for visiting specialists, typed correspondence, and booked transportation requests for patients and their families.

Bombay General Hospital, Bombay, India
Hospital Admitting Clerk, 1980 - 1984
Admitted patients to Emergency Room facility, recorded nature of emergency and personal history and advised attending physicians on the status of each patient.

Interests

Reading, walking, cooking Indian cuisine.

References

Furnished upon request.

Patricia J. Drennen

4365 Berkshire Drive, Apt. 6
Warren, Ohio 44484
216/555-1234

Objective

Seeking a position that will enable me to utilize a wide variety of secretarial skills.

Education

Kent State University, Trumbull Branch, Warren, Ohio
1997 -- Successfully completed courses in IBM Word Processing and Medical Insurance.

Employment

Casper's Weight Loss Clinic, Warren, Ohio
May 1997 - June 2000
Temporary Counselor
Filled in while permanent counselor/secretary was on leave; duties included counseling clients and promoting sales along with extensive secretarial, receptionist, and office duties.

Trumbull County Courthouse, Warren, Ohio
September 1964 - June 1967
Deputy Clerk
Reported to Sheriff T. Herbert Thomas; responsible for producing legal documents in addition to performing a wide variety of administrative duties.

The Grinnel Corporation, Warren, Ohio
September 1963 - September 1964
Secretary
Acted as combination receptionist/secretary/teletype operator. Performed a wide range of clerical and office duties for engineering department.

Skills

Typing and current word processing skills, excellent oral and written communication skills, organization skills, and a proven ability to work well with people.

Extracurricular

Chairperson of various school and athletic committees, 1973 - 1996
Member of Beta Sigma Phi Sorority, 1982 - 1992
Offices Held: Secretary, 1983 - 1985; Recording Secretary, 1986

References

Available upon request.

Sandra L. Gardiner

81 Huntington Lane • Buffalo, NY 11456 • Cellular: 716-555-7849

Objective

To secure a challenging position in sales and sales management.

Work Experience

The GAP Clothing Store, Erieview Mall, Erie, PA
   Manager: 1995 - 1998
   Duties: Supervised 8 full-time and 3 part-time employees.
   Interviewed and hired sales employees. Conducted training seminars for sales force.

Kaufman's Department Store, Erie, PA
   Sales Clerk: 1994 - 1995
   Duties: Sold merchandise, assisted buyer on trips to purchase stock.

Qualifications & Awards

- Extensive knowledge of sales techniques and the ability to train staff employees to utilize these techniques effectively.
- Received Sales Person of the Month award for nine consecutive months while employed at Kaufman's.
- Awarded Top Manager status for highest sales revenue for a GAP store in the eastern division in 1998.

Related Experience

- Contributed written articles on sales techniques for the *Sales Review Quarterly*.
- Codirected a five-day intensive sales seminar for retail sales training offered annually at the GAP training school in Philadelphia.

Professional Membership

Association of Retail Managers, Erie, PA
   Office held: President, 1996 - 1998

Additional

Willing to travel. References furnished upon request.

Carl Pujol   *Photographer*

22-B W. 44th Street
Wilmington, Delaware 19835
302-555-9080
carl_pujol@xxx.com

Education
- Cooper Union, New York City, M.A. Photography, 2000
- New York University Tisch School of the Arts, B.A. Photography, 1993

Objective
To secure employment as a fashion photographer for a major magazine

Experience
1998 - present
Self-employed photographer
- Developed a profitable portrait business
- Designed and shot record album cover for the rock group Dream Scape
- Hired to photograph models for the book *Men* by Sandcastle Productions
- Assisted head photographer in Havana, Cuba, for a documentary developed in London by Wildcat Productions

1995 - 1998
Photographer
Sears, Chicago, Illinois
- Assisted head photographer in all aspects of shooting print work for the 1995 and 1996 catalogues
- Promoted to head photographer 1997
- Designed, shot, and developed 1997 and 1998 catalogues
- Resigned to attend a special invitational fashion photo class in London

1993-1996
Photographers assistant
Victoria's Secret, London, England
- Designed and shot 50 percent of the 1995 autumn portfolio
- Shot and developed 50 percent of the 1996 spring portfolio
- Assisted team in developing marketing strategies and campaigns

Demonstrated Skills
- Ability to work under pressure and meet deadlines
- Ability to work independently or collaborate

References
Furnished upon request.

IDA LOPEZ
1740 PALMETTO DRIVE
ORLANDO, FL 32816
(305) 555-1173

OBJECTIVE
To utilize my problem-solving and communication skills in a credit agency that offers management potential.

EDUCATION
University of Central Florida, Orlando FL
M.B.A. program. 9/00 - present.
University of Florida, Gainesville, FL.
Major: Accounting 1973

VOLUNTEER EXPERIENCE
10/97 - 7/00
Psychiatric Institute, Orlando, FL.
Member of a team that included psychologists and psychiatrists.
- Implemented treatment plans.
- Observed patients and reported meaningful symptomatic behavior to professional staff.
- Engaged in therapeutic activities with patients.
- Influenced patients' treatment by offering emotional support.

EMPLOYMENT EXPERIENCE
Macys, Orlando, FL
Assistant Credit Manager, 11/78 - 2/82
- Assisted in the development and implementation of a credit policy for the store.
- Managed all aspects of store accounts.
- Engaged in collection activities and increased earnings by 48 percent.
- Prepared reports making specific recommendations to management.

Paul Harper Men's Wear, Inc., Orlando, FL
Credit Counselor, 7/73 - 11/78.
- Interviewed and counseled customers applying for credit.
- Evaluated income information and made decisions regarding credit lines.
- Investigated credit histories for any discrepancies.

ATTRIBUTES
Willingness to work nights and weekends.
Ability to influence others and achieve desired outcome.

REFERENCES
Furnished upon request.

YLON SANDLER

755 Alexandria Street, #5W   **202-555-7722**
Washington, DC 20013   **sandler@xxx.com**

Career Objective
A position as archivist or curator for the federal government.

Education
Georgetown University, Washington, DC, M.A. Anthropology, 1993
Columbia University, New York, NY, B.A. Anthropology, 1992 GPA 4.0

Skills
Fluent in Spanish, Swahili, and Zulu
Specialist in ancient documents

Relevant Experience
1998 - 2000
Freelance tour guide -- Kenya, Mali
• Organized and led tours through national parks in Africa
• Provided historical and cultural information
• Arranged opportunities for group members to accomplish goals
• Intervened in and resolved crises

Employment Experience
1993 - 1998
Archivist, Smithsonian Institute, Washington, DC
• Searched for, acquired, analyzed, classified, catalogued, restored, exhibited, maintained, and stored historical documents
• Planned and conducted educational programs
• Determined the amount and type of material to be exhibited

References
Available upon request

marlena comninel

22 South Avon Street
Charleston, South Carolina 29411
Home: (435) 555-2238
Pager: (435) 555-7773

objective
To return to the field of audiology in a major medical center

education
Stanford University, Palo Alto, California -- M.A. Audiology, 1970
Duke University, Durham, North Carolina -- B.A. Psychology, 1968

activities
Lived in Nauplia, Greece; 1991 - 2001
Attended the Center for Social Planning; studied Anthropology and Psychology.
Volunteered at the local church to counsel adults with hearing loss.
Led hiking groups through the Pindus Mountains of Northern Greece.

employment
1970 - 1991
Durham Eye and Ear Hospital, Durham, North Carolina; Audiologist
Provided direct clinical services to patients with communication disorders.
This included testing, evaluation, and treatment.

accomplishments
- Developed and conducted community-based hearing-protection programs.
- Administered community outreach activities.
- Supervised three audiologists and five administrative assistants.
- Counseled individuals and families about hearing disorders.
- Taught behavioral techniques to improve communication.
- Consulted with Fortune 500 companies regarding the development of hearing conservation programs.
- Served as assistant editor of *Hear*, a publication of the Southern California Hearing Council.

associations
American Speech and Hearing Association
American Academy of Audiologists

certification
Certificate of Clinical Competence

references
Available upon request

JACK PHILLIPS
978 North Bend
Iowa City, Iowa 52240
(319) 555-8403 jphillips@xxx.com

- ## OBJECTIVE

Project management position in a food product or agricultural supply company.

- ## EDUCATION

University of Iowa, Iowa City
M.S. in Agriculture, 1995
B.S. in Agriculture, 1993

- ## AGRICULTURE/PEACE CORPS EXPERIENCE

Served in Mali. 1999 - 2001
- Administered research and development programs.
- Applied approved methods of enhancing quantity and quality of farm corps.
- Managed production operations.
- Increased yields with less labor.
- Utilized safe and effective pest control procedures.

- ## EMPLOYMENT EXPERIENCE

Iowa state agricultural research station. 1995 - 1999
- Developed procedures to improve the quality of farm animals and crops.
- Supervised 3 employees.
- Coordinated all agronomic operations.

- ## HONORS

Graduated *cum laude* 1993, 1995
Dean's List 1989 - 1993

- ## REFERENCES

Available upon request.

Dwight Miller

3425 East Broad Street
Columbus, Ohio 43213
(614) 555-9078

Experience

1998 - present
Self-employed automobile mechanic

1995 - 1998
S&W Auto, Columbus, Ohio
Auto Mechanic/Manager

- Produced and implemented performance and quality development program
- Established additional efficiency and reliability standards
- Improved response time of repairs by 2 days
- Improved customer service by cutting costs and reducing prices
- Changed company image to that of a reputable, dependable neighborhood auto repair shop
- Increased client accounts by 60 percent

1989 - 1995   Texaco Auto Service
Auto Mechanic

Education

1988 - 1990   Cooperative Technical Education Institute for Automobile
Mechanics Columbus, Ohio

1986 - 1988   Columbus Community College
Courses in Marketing, Economics, Customer Relations, Advertising, Accounting

1981 - 1986   Samuel Gomper's High School for Vocational Training

References furnished upon request

Jason McAllister

7723 West 15th Street • Sacramento, CA 95814 • Cellular: (916) 555-9992

Objective

To use my decision making, problem solving, and persuasive skills in a sales management position.

Education

University of California at Berkeley
Berkeley, CA 1975
B.A. in Business and Marketing; GPA 3.9

Skills

Results oriented
Strong persuasive ability
Proven fund-raising capability
Powerful management skills
Ability to solve problems and overcome objections

Related Experience

1985 - present
Catholic Church
- Organized work force to raise funds for Father Moon's organization. These efforts resulted in a 60 percent increase in revenue over a 10-year period.
- Persuaded more than 200 people to join the church
- Reorganized many of the activities of the church that resulted in more programs at ⅓ the cost
- Presided over liturgical functions
- Attended to the moral and educational needs of the members
- Supervised numerous projects

Professional Experience

1976 - 1985
Phillips Electronics - Berkeley, CA
Sales Representative
- Developed systems to provide product information supported by company-backed action
- Promoted sales through pricing restraints and the development of strategies and programs. Store income increased by 30 percent
- Created new markets for our products
- Formulated new product lines to reflect consumer needs

References enclosed

John Von Hamer

963 Lake Drive
Philadelphia, PA 19104
Home: (215) 555-5352
Pager: (215) 555-8890

Experience

Small appliance mechanic - Self-employed (1995 - present)
Repair cords, connections, and switches.
Replace plugs and install terminals of all types.
Adjust, repair, or replace temperature controls.
Analyze the performance of compressors, dehumidifiers, humidifiers, and air conditioners.
Restore switching circuits, thermostats, relays, solid state components, and SCR.

Warehouse Foreman - The Seamack Corporation (1985 - 1995)
Managed 85,000 square-foot facility.
Supervised 30 employees.

Achievements

Increased storage capacity by 15 percent.
Expanded warehouse output by 10 percent.
Designed and implemented new inventory procedures.
Promoted to foreman in 1989.
Named supervisor of the year for three consecutive years.

Education

Washington High School for Electronics
Completed 10 seminars in personnel management.

References

Furnished upon request.

Guideon Sol

Present address
56 Emek Refaim
2192 Jerusalem, Israel
0019722 555-823

Permanent address
2192 Beverly Rd.
Springfield, MA 01109
413-555-9974

Objective

To work for the United Nations as a translator

Education

Fulbright scholarship to study Hebrew literature and religion 1998 - 2000,
University of Jerusalem
M.A. Hebrew and Theology, 2000, Exchange Program, Boston University,
Division of Religious and Theological Studies, Boston, MA
B.A. French, 1993, Universite Laval, Sainte-Foy, Quebec, Canada,
Summa Cum Laude

Languages

French, Hebrew, Patois, Spanish, Portuguese

Employment History

1995 - 1998 University of Quebec at Montreal, ESL Instructor.
1993 - 1995 Lycee A. Petion, Port-Au-Prince, Haiti, ESL Instructor

Created ESL Program. Designed and developed a challenging curricula that included grammar, vocabulary, and reading. Taught advanced courses in American Literature. Instructed beginning, intermediate, and advanced conversational English courses. Designed survey instruments to ascertain student's experiences, expectations, and difficulties with English. Counseled students about scholarships and study in America. Coordinated student activities. Facilitated a cross-cultural group that met weekly. Sponsored several cross-cultural programs.

Achievements

Offered full-time tenure position at the Universite Laval
Recipient of Fulbright Scholarship

Strengths

Ability to work with diverse populations.
Excellent language and communication skills.
Significant teaching ability with various student groups.
Ability and strong interest in assisting others.

Nancy Mantello

6 Horizon Road
Whindham, Ohio 44288
216-555-9361

Related Experience

<u>Treasurer, Board of Directors, Horizon House, Whindham, Ohio</u>
1994 - present
- Conserved $80,000 on air-conditioning cooling towers
- Arranged a 15-year warranty on building's roof
- Brought about the reduction of $2,000,000 escrow mortgage currency
- Reviewed and changed the specifications of the contract award for fire-doors
- Produced substantial savings in the employees' health insurance package
- Promoted positive action on the lighting in Riverbank Park, as a consequence of an excellent relationship with the mayor and town council members

Work History

<u>Office Manager, Land O' Lakes, Inc., Kent, Ohio</u>
1978 - 1993
- Supervised a clerical staff of 17
- Prepared quarterly and annual reports, tax returns, payroll, and warehouse stock replenishment statistics
- Directed computerized stock reconciliation and rotation processes
- Conducted cash flow, securities analysis, and project feasibility studies
- Prepared and directed yearly management seminars
- Received several promotions after starting at the company as a clerk

<u>Clerk, Giant Eagle, Inc., Warren, Ohio</u>
1969 - 1978
- Supervised and controlled large amounts of cash flow
- Maintained weekly ledgers
- Computed figures with speed and accuracy
- Maintained activity in customer accounts

Education

Youngstown State University, Youngstown, Ohio
Courses included Accounting, Business, Typing, and Dictation

References on request

SAMUEL J. CLARK

159 Edgewater Drive
Lexington, Kentucky 40502
(606) 555-1947
sam_clark@xxx.com

EXPERIENCE

OVERDO PRODUCTIONS, Lexington, KY -- September 1993 - present
Volunteer
In addition to providing administrative support for this radio production company, I write grant proposals and edit scripts and books for broadcast.

PACIFICA-WBKI 99.5 FM, Lexington, KY -- July 1988 - September 1993
Coordinator and Associate Producer
Recruited, trained, and supervised 400 volunteers. Responsible for writing and producing on-air recruitment announcements and soliciting in-kind donations. Proceeds exceeded $20 million. Researched subjects related to health and social issues and coordinated guests for live on-air discussions on various topics.

THE METROPOLITAN MUSEUM OF ART, New York -- November 1995 - August 1987
Accounting Clerk
Processed payments to vendors and investigated complaints and discrepancies between invoices and receiving reports. Resolved conflicts using customer service and critical-thinking skills.

TEACHING EXPERIENCE

NEW YORK CITY BOARD OF EDUCATION -- September 1997 - June 1999
Instructor
Instructed culturally diverse populations in reading and English at John F. Kennedy and South Bronx High Schools.

ROCHESTER MUSEUM AND SCIENCE CENTER -- January 1986 - August 1987
Instructor
Taught educational workshops in science using film, photography, written materials, and museum artifacts.

EDUCATION

EASTERN KENTUCKY UNIVERSITY, Richmond, KY
Specialized in Speech Pathology; Post Baccalaureate, 20 credits; B.A. English, 1983

References available on request

JESSICA NATHAN

87948 Fairview Place • Huntsville, Alabama 35804
Home: (205) 555-9856 • Pager: (205) 555-0014

OBJECTIVE   Psychiatric social work position in an adolescent treatment facility

RELATED EXPERIENCE

FOSTER PARENT

- Care for hard-to-place children. Accepted the extraordinary challenges of raising handicapped children and achieved dramatic improvements. Patiently and diligently encouraged independence and self-reliance with valuable results.
- Volunteered to participate in TEAM, a post-placement support group.
- Provided special classes, guidance, and psychological care for foster parents and children.
- Participated in training programs sponsored by the Huntsville Society for the Crippled and Disabled.

PSYCHIATRIC INSTITUTE OF HUNTSVILLE
1989-1998 Psychiatric Social Worker

- Developed individual and group counseling treatment programs for teens with a history of violent behavior
- Coordinated a teen drama program in conjunction with the Creative Arts Team
- Initiated a substance abuse program in coordination with NA and AA
- Coauthored six articles relating to adolescence, published variously in regional and national publications
- Planned supportive services to ease return to the community

EDUCATION

University of Knoxville, Knoxville, TN
M.S.W. 1988
B.A. Psychology 1986
C.S.W. 1980

References available on request

ERIC COLLIER

8354 South Dixie Drive
North Miami Beach, Florida 33160
E-mail: ecollier@xxx.com
(305) 555-7658

OBJECTIVE

A position as tax attorney in a firm located in North Miami

EDUCATION

Yale Law School, Ph.D. Law 1957
Yale University, B.S. History 1954

SIGNIFICANT ACHIEVEMENTS

Worked with Mario Cuomo to establish the United Nations fund
for Latin American Children.

Developed and chaired the Matthew McAustin Foundation for the Arts.

Represented Nancy Carnegie in her opposition to development of Newberland Wand
in Georgia. A 1983 legal decision preserved the area under the National Park Service.

Legal advisor to the New York Mets, 1970 - 1989

Negotiated the acquisition of two textbook concerns: Rinehart and Company and John
C. Winston, 1959

Became a partner in the Wall Street firm of Wilson, Carter and Mills in 1958. Contin-
ued with this firm until 1990.

VOLUNTEER EXPERIENCE

International Executive Service Corps, Stamford, Connecticut

Served as consultant to developing international businesses in Iran, South Korea,
Columbia, and Peru.

REFERENCES ARE AVAILABLE UPON REQUEST.

KELLY GRAVES

777 South Main Street • Sweetwater, Tennessee 88485
Cellular: (615) 555-9805 • Pager: (615) 555-6674

OBJECTIVE

To administer a social service agency handling psychiatric patients.

RELATED EXPERIENCE

1997 - 2000
- Founded an advocacy group for emotionally disturbed adolescents called Community Action for Teens.
- Cofounded the Peer Power Coalition that provided former mental patients with the tools to become a political force.
- Wrote grant proposals that led to $200,000 in financing from the state and private organizations for the Peer Specialist Training Center to train former patients to help others like themselves.

PROFESSIONAL EXPERIENCE

Administrator, Children's Aid Society, Dallas, Texas
1993 - 1999
- Established a new computer system
- Supervised 22 employees
- Wrote grant proposals that increased revenues by $3.6 million
- Developed training programs designed to advance interest in our procedures and policies
- Managed a budget of one million dollars
- Resigned to participate in advocacy work for psychiatric patients

Administrator, Washington Square Institute for Psychotherapy and Mental Health, Dallas, Texas
1985 - 1993
- Reorganized systems for recruiting and selecting professional and clerical personnel.
- Developed a training program that earned a superior reputation.
- Successfully prepared and administered operating and capital budgets of two million dollars.

Administrative assistant, St. Johns Hospital-Psychiatric Institute, Dallas, Texas
1981 - 1985
- Wrote grant proposals resulting in revenues that increased patient services by 80 percent.

EDUCATION

Midwestern State University, Wichita Falls, Texas
- M.B.A. 1980
- B.A. 1977 - Business

References available upon request

KATRINA LEVOFSKY

18 Cavendish Drive
Madison, WI 53714
Klevofsky@xxx.com
(608) 555-3332

EDUCATION

Ph.D. Clinical Psychology, Marquette University, Milwaukee, WI, 1993
Dissertation topic: "The Analytic Attitude and Its Effect on Women."
B.S. Psychology, University of Toronto, Ontario, Canada, 1987

PROFILE

- Traveled extensively to study parenthood as a developmental phase in African and Asian cultures, 1997 - present.
- Book will be published by Harper and Row 2003.

EXPERIENCE

University of Wisconsin, Oshkosh, Wisconsin
- Sabbatical, 1997 - 1998
- Assistant Professor, Department of Psychology, 1993 - 1997
- Taught graduate courses in Abnormal and Developmental Psychology.
- Developed and taught undergraduate courses in Introductory Psychology.

PUBLICATIONS

(1994) *Parenthood as a Developmental Phase.* New York: International Universities Press.

(1995) "Mourning and the Birth of a Disabled Child." *Journal of American Psychoanalytic Association* 8, 389-416.

(1996) "The Narcissistic Determinants of Professional Artists: A Portrait of Five Female Artists" *Psychiatry*, 33: 454-456.

PROFESSIONAL ASSOCIATIONS

- American Psychoanalytic Association
- The Freudian Society of Wisconsin
- Women in Science

REFERENCES

Available upon request

MARIA CARVELLE
167 East Flamingo Road • Las Vegas, Nevada 88675 • (702) 555-4433

EXPERIENCE

- Researched, reviewed, and verified rent invoices for office leases
- Monitored lease renewals, terminations, and option dates
- Compiled data for Administrative Space Requisitions
- Arranged and managed commercial real estate closings
- Organized and administered title closings
- Summarized leases and revised rent rolls of commercial properties for financial analysis package
- Formed corporate entities and drafted certificates of incorporation
- Updated records, prepared by-laws, and drafted special resolutions
- Managed ten midsize strip centers that included maintenance, tenant relations, and rent collection
- Developed an advertising campaign to lease vacant space in strip centers, resulting in all available space being rented.
- Assisted in producing the 1999 International Shopping Convention

EMPLOYMENT HISTORY

- Real Estate Administrator 2/98 - 4/99, Sprint International Inc., New York, NY
- Legal Administrative Assistant 9/97 - 2/98, Marchall, Tulley, and Jones, New York, NY
- Legal Assistant 9/93 - 8/97, Kiwi Management, Inc., Bogota, NJ
- Assistant Director of Property Management 11/88 - 9/93, The Hill Group, New York, NY
- Legal Assistant 2/86 - 11/88, Hal T. Rose, P.C., New York, NY

EDUCATION

N.Y.U. Real Estate Institute 1987 - 1993
Courses in real estate sales, transactions, syndication, and tax laws
Brooklyn College, City University of New York -- B.A. History, 1983

LICENSES/SKILLS

Broker's license, Notary Public
Microsoft Word, Acces, Excel, and PowerPoint

References available on request

Carmen Perez
c/o Cruz
1693 Collins Avenue
Miami, Florida 33239
315-555-2132

Career Ambition
To work in the public library system

Education
University of Havana, Havana, Cuba,
M.S. in Library Science 1987
B.A. in Foreign Languages 1985

Computer Skills
Presently attending Florida State College continuing education classes for Lotus
Software: CLIPPER, BRIEF, UNIX
Hardware: IBM PC-XT, AST 486/25

Employment History
Emigrated to the United States, August 1994

Main Library, Havana, Cuba, Head Librarian June 1987 - August 1994

- Managed the Main Library
- Supervised staff of 20 workers
- Instituted computer cataloguing system
- Working with a limited budget, brought current literature, periodicals, and audio-visual materials to Cuba
- Developed a continuing education library program, in which leading Latin authors read from their works
- Created a reading program for children
- Developed and coordinated a Great Books group

References are enclosed

AMY RANDALL

4967 Front Street
Gallup, New Mexico 87321
(505) 555-7761
E-mail: randall@xxx.com

GOAL

A position as food and service manager.

EDUCATION

B.A. Hotel Management, University of Santa Fe, New Mexico, 1982

ACCOMPLISHMENTS

1998 - present
- Created recipes that appeared in the 1998 *New York Times Cookbook*
- Taught adult education cooking courses
- Entered and won several cooking contests
- Created and sold recipes for:
  Green bean walnut pate
  Carrot yam soup
  Salmon in ginger-soy sauce
  Sauteed spinach with garlic and red pepper
  Semolina pizza with zucchini and pesto topping
  Gluten-free pizza with onions, rosemary, and roasted garlic
- Competed for a cooking program on a major TV network

CAREER EXPERIENCES

1990 - 1998   Hilton Hotel, Santa Fe, New Mexico
Food and beverage manager
- Directed the food services for the hotel manager
- Supervised the operation of the hotel's restaurants and banquet facilities
- Scheduled and supervised food and beverage preparation
- Directed the work of 32 service workers
- Planned meals, estimated costs, and ordered supplies

1982 - 1990   Comfort Inn, Santa Fe, New Mexico
Assistant to F&B manager
- Assisted in training and supervising the food service staff
- Inspected hotel's restaurant and banquet facilities
- Planned menu
- Directed food supply office

REFERENCES AVAILABLE UPON REQUEST

Bridget Wilson

1221 Spencer Street
Hartford, Connecticut 06489
(203) 555-8979   bwilson@xxx.com

OBJECTIVE

A position as operations manager

PROFESSIONAL HISTORY

1997 - 2001   Connecticut Paper Company -- Stamford, CT
                Operations manager

1986 - 1997   Smithe-Johnson Paper Company -- Burlington, VT
                Promoted from staff accountant to operations manager

1983 - 1986   SFV Paper -- Hartford, CT
                Accountant

AREA OF EXPERTISE

Accounting/Finance Management

SELECTED ACCOMPLISHMENTS

Prepared an operations budget of $22 million. Reorganized accounting system that provided superior analysis of profits. Introduced controls to safeguard assets. Maintained profitability at 30 percent above industry norms. Reviewed and recommended changes in company operations resulting in 50 percent greater efficiency. Managed the elimination of two divisions, saving the company $3 million.

RECENT ACCOMPLISHMENTS

Volunteer, Stevens Center for Eating Disorders
After overcoming my own eating disorder, became a volunteer to help others. Collaborated with professional therapists, physicians, nurses, and dietitians to provide coordinated comprehensive care. Developed and presented educational programs in local schools, and offered nutritional counseling. Wrote an article about eating disorders that was published in the local paper.

References available upon request

HOWARD FOX

10 MAYFAIR BOULEVARD
BURLINGTON, VT 05401
Home: (802) 555-1138
Pager: (802) 555-9224

OBJECTIVE: To obtain employment as an interior decorator

EDUCATION: UNIVERSITY OF OREGON, EUGENE, OREGON
Major: Communications. B.A. 1994
Minor: Art

ART STUDENTS GUILD, EUGENE, OREGON
Courses: Free Hand and Mechanical Drawing, Space Planning,
Residential Design, History of Great Interiors, and Fabric Design.

EXPERIENCE: 1998 - present
FREELANCE INTERIOR DESIGN CONSULTANT
- Prepare room layouts, color schemes, wall and window treatments.
- Supervise the installation of lighting, carpeting, and cabinets.
- Occasionally hang wall paper, install lighting and cabinets.
- Design architectural details such as crown molding.
- Compile presentation folders of fabric, wallpaper, and wood finish
  samples; prices, and competing products.

1994 - 1998
LYNN MERRILL TEMPORARY AGENCY, EUGENE, OREGON
TEMP WORKER FOR WBSI RADIO
- Maintained news service machines.
- Collected and distributed audio feeds to news editors and writers.
- Scheduled guests. Operated tape recorder.
- Assisted in scheduling, coordinating, and setting up productions.

KFAA TV
- Assisted the technical director with lighting, taping, and sound work.

CENTER FOR CREATIVE PHOTOGRAPHY
- Prepared all lighting and equipment.
- Planned layout content and spacing of 23 projects.

ACHIEVEMENTS: Offered full-time position at WBSI Radio
Graduated *summa cum laude*
Finalist in a U.S. Photography competition

References available on request

JOAN KARLSON

456 West 107th Street • New York, NY 10025 • (212) 555-7788

OBJECTIVE

To obtain a position that will utilize my talents and interests.

EDUCATION

New York University, Master of Arts, Psychology
Graduated 1989

City College, City University of New York.
Bachelor of Arts, Early Childhood Education
Graduated *cum laude* 1987

EXPERIENCE

2000 - Present
Developed and managed a family day care program for 5 youngsters in my home.
- Planned and coordinated an instructional program that provided for the social, emotional, intellectual, and physical needs of children.
- Established goals and evaluated progress.
- Utilized stimulating activities such as creative storytelling, arts, and cooking.
- Created instructional lesson plans to enhance decision-making skills.
- Enlisted skilled volunteers in the areas of music and art.

1/95 - 6/00
Bank Street College, New York, NY
Adjunct Lecturer. Department of Education.
- Instructor for three undergraduate courses in early childhood education.

9/90 - 1/95
NYC Board of Education
Teacher, Common Branch
- Taught kindergarten through third grade.

PROFESSIONAL ACCREDITATION

New York State Certification, Common Branch.

REFERENCES

Available upon request.

A n d r e s   S i m m s

101 Winston Way • Raleigh, N.C. 27706

Cellular: (919) 555-8778 • E-mail: Asimms@xxx.com

EDUCATION

MBA, Duke University, 1990
BS, Industrial Engineering, Duke University, 1987
Minor in Theater Arts

OBJECTIVE

*To utilize my managerial, communication, and problem-solving skills in an
engineering position that offers a high level of responsibility.*

RELATED EXPERIENCE

Theater for the New City, New York, NY, 1999 - 2001
Directed and coproduced six contemporary plays.

Sandcastle Players, Inc., New York, NY, 1997 - 1999
Directed staged readings and contemporary plays.

WORK EXPERIENCE

Corning Cookware, Ithaca, NY, 1990 - 1997
Industrial Engineer
- Designed personal computing software technology.
- Developed management control systems to aid in financial planning and cost
  analysis.
- Conceived and implemented production plans to control product quality.
- Designed job performance evaluation programs.

MEMBERSHIPS/ASSOCIATIONS

Industrial Engineering Society

REFERENCES

Available upon request.

JOEL S. COHEN

112 Anderson Avenue
Cliffside Park, NJ 07010
Home: (201) 555-8667
Cellular: (201) 555-1243

OBJECTIVE

To utilize my communication, problem-solving, and decision-making skills in conjunction with my knowledge of the law in relation to tenant-landlord issues.

EDUCATION

Bachelor of Arts in Music, June 1976
Rutgers, New Brunswick, NJ

EXPERIENCE

President, Tenants Union 4/96 - present
- Organized tenants of 112 Anderson Avenue.
- Performed detailed legal research.
- Conducted interviews.
- Prepared documents and correspondence.
- Succeeded in winning rebates three times in two years.
- Elected president last three years.
- Negotiated landlord-tenant disputes.
- Created "Anderson Avenue Newsletter."

Music Teacher   9/86-6/97
MANHATTAN SCHOOL OF MUSIC, New York, NY
- Taught courses in piano and guitar.
- Coordinated student events.
- Supervised student teachers.

Music Teacher   9/76-9/86
JULLIARD, New York, NY
- Taught undergraduate courses in piano.
- Organized yearly special events.

REFERENCES

Available upon request

TINA JONES

31 Bay Drive • Chicago, IL 60641 • (312) 555-6655

EXPERIENCE

8/95 - 5/00
Dwight Correctional Center, Dwight, IL
Pattern Maker

- Received training in fine tailoring and alterations.
- Developed expertise in pattern cutting and design.
- Created a line of women's wear retailed by three major stores in Dwight, IL

9/92 - 6/95
Bay Drive High School student

EDUCATION

Correspondence courses in Liberal Arts
Dwight Community College
GED, 1998

SKILLS

- Organized and co-led self-help group.
- Wrote and published inmate newspaper.
- Trained and supervised five inmates in reporting, editing, and layout.

INTERESTS

Member of the DCC Choir

References enclosed

Burt Abzug

2341 Forest Place
St. Louis, MO 63130
(314) 555-6411
Abzug@xxx.com

Occupational Goal

Full-time employment as a Commercial Artist.

Activities and Awards

Created the layout for the "Forest Place Newsletter."

- Selected type, drawings, photos, inks, and the printing process.
- Provided my own illustrations and hand-lettering designs.
- Interviewed and directed the work of two photographers.
- Supervised the entire project for three years.
- Awarded "Highest Achievement for Community Service."

Employment Experience

Carpenter-Johnson Construction Company, St. Louis, MO
1980 - 2000.
Retired due to injury on the job.

- Cut, fit, and assembled wood and other materials in the construction
  of single family homes and apartments.
- Installed trim, molding, cabinets, doors, and paneling.
- Coordinated construction activities with workers in other trades.
- Adjusted blueprints when necessary.

Carpenter Apprentice, Carpentry Joint Apprenticeship Committee.
1977 - 1980

References available upon request.

Edward Hanover

396 Colorado Avenue • Idaho Falls, Idaho 83402 • Cellular: (208) 555-6744

OBJECTIVE

To offer my expertise in advertising to a large agency on the West Coast

VOLUNTEER EXPERIENCE

EARTHWATCH, 2000 - 2001
EASTERN CARPATHIANS BIOSPHERE, POLAND

- Accompanied Drs. Karlsen, Vasquez, and Phillips
- Hiked up to 10 kilometers/day
- Observed and tracked large mammals with radio telemetry
- Captured deer and large predators
- Analyzed brown-bear habitat
- Collected vegetation data

BELIZE'S BARRIER REEF
TOBACCO CAVE, BELIZE

- Accompanied Dr. Y. Schwartz
- Studied how reef communities function and maintain species diversity
- Analyzed habitats and conducted visual fish surveys
- Used scuba equipment to lay down transects to census certain fish and quantify plants
- Monitored coral recruitment and growth rates

EXPERIENCE IN ADVERTISING

MCINTIRE, JAMISON ADVERTISING AGENCY, 1986 - 1998
BOISE, IDAHO
EXECUTIVE CREATIVE DIRECTOR

- Enlivened and energized the creative culture of the agency
- Created a distinct identity to overhaul all aspects of operations
- Revamped strategic planning
- Increased revenue from $710 million to $960 million
- Supervised work on accounts of blue-chip clients that included Black and Decker, Nabisco, Ivory soap, Campbell's, and 7-Eleven
- Tutored executive ranks on using new state-of-the-art computer programming technology

EDUCATION

YALE UNIVERSITY, NEW HAVEN, CT -- MBA 1986
UNIVERSITY OF CALIFORNIA, BERKELEY -- BA BUSINESS 1984
Graduated *cum laude*

KATHLEEN McCORNICK

124 Bay Drive • Chicago, IL 60641
(312) 555-7622 • K_McCornick@xxx.com

OBJECTIVE

To obtain a position as a Public Relations Specialist in order to apply my knowledge of promotional and fundraising activities.

RELEVANT EXPERIENCE

Volunteer
The Church of Saint Anthony, 1992 - 1999
Prepared and promoted annual church functions.
Organized recruitment program.
Trained and directed volunteers.
Evaluated annual reports and income statements.
Directed fundraising activities that increased income by 40 percent.

Public Relations Executive
Ruder Finn and Rotman, Inc., Chicago, IL, 1987 - 1992
Drafted budgets and projects for numerous corporations.
Publicized major events.
Developed promotional strategies to support specific marketing objectives.

EDUCATION

B.A., Journalism, 1986
Graduate courses in Public Relations
University of Illinois at Urbana/Champaign

ASSOCIATIONS

The Public Relations Society of America

References available on request.

MARK NUSSBAUM

153 Main Street   Home: (718) 555-5411
Flushing, NY 11367   Pager: (718) 555-7990

CAREER OBJECTIVE: *To secure employment as a travel consultant in an agency that offers advancement opportunities.*

ACTIVITIES: Homemaker
                      Dec. 1994 - present
                      Five years experience raising triplets.
                      • Organized and managed daily routines.
                      • Scheduled educational and play activities.
                      • Prepared meals.
                      • Studied numerous psychology books.
                      • Developed patience, insight, and understanding.

EMPLOYMENT HISTORY: Travel Consultant
                      Aug. 1992 - Dec. 1994
                      F.L.Y. Travel Agency, New York, NY
                      • Arranged conventions for major corporations.
                      • Organized entertainment and recreational activities.
                      • Planned sightseeing trips.
                      • Negotiated with hotels for group room and meal rates.
                      • Prepared efficient and economical business travel plans.

                      Reservation Specialist
                      July 1985 - August 1992
                      TWA Airlines, Peoria, IL
                      • Handled customer requests using World Span computer system.
                      • Arranged hotel and car rental accommodations.
                      • Computed fares.
                      • Resolved disputes.

EDUCATION: B.A. Psychology, Rockford College, 1985

FOREIGN LANGUAGES: Hebrew, French.

REFERENCES: *Available on request.*

IRA SCHWARTZ

212 West 13th Street
New York, NY 10011
(212) 555-9998

OBJECTIVE

To obtain a position in construction engineering.

EDUCATION

New York University, New York, NY
M.S., Civil Engineering, 1990

Hunter College, City University of NY
B.S., Civil Engineering, 1989

SPECIAL SKILLS

International Chess Master
- Won major chess tournaments
- New York Open -- 1993, 1994
- World Open -- 1991, 1993, 1994
- Albany Open -- 1991

Taught chess classes in three NYC elementary schools.
Sponsored by the PTA (1993-1994).
Captain - Hunter College Chess Team
- Coached team members
- Organized tournaments including travel
- Promoted the team via simultaneous exhibitions throughout the city

ENGINEERING EXPERIENCE

6/90 - 6/91   New York Department of Transportation, Albany, NY
            Assistant Engineer
- Inspected the construction of reinforced concrete bridges and roadways
- Provided recommendations to contractors that were implemented
- Assisted in the design of roadways and associated structures
- Responsible for hydrologic aspects of highway design

REGISTRATION

Certified Engineer in Training, 1991

AFFILIATIONS

American Society of Civil Engineers
U.S. Chess Federation

References available on request.

ROBERT LINDSEY

77 Hansbright Street • Boston, Massachusetts 02169
(617) 555-1423 • lindsey@xxx.com

Objective	To utilize proven skills in direct marketing
Education	M.A. Marketing, 1986, University of Massachusetts, Boston, MA. B.A. English, 1985, Boston University, Boston, MA.
Specific Strengths	I have spent the past two years caring for someone who was extremely ill. Specific strengths that enabled me to take responsibility for this person were: an eagerness to accomplish goals; a take-charge personality; patience and compassion; willingness to work hard; dedication.
Technical Ability	Languages: Basic, Cobol, CICS, Fortran, Pascal, C Plus Environments: DOS, VM/CMS Data Base Management Systems: IMAGE, IDMS

Career Experience

DATABASE AMERICA, Boston, MA
Account Executive, 1989 - 2000

- Sold creative services through cold calling. Concentrated on direct mail programs and corporate information kits.
- Generated new business that increased sales 26 percent with Sony Corporation, Bell Atlantic Information Systems, Bell Atlantic Mobile Division, and Medical Economics Publishing.
- Sold managed lists plus business and consumer compiled files to list brokers, mailers, and advertising agencies.
- Responsible for all communication on the largest managed files.
- Directed all aspects of direct marketing campaigns.

BRC INC., Boston, MA
Account Executive, 1986 - 1989

- Developed new client base: McGraw-Hill Professional and Reference Division, McGraw-Hill Health Division, Prentice Hall
- Dow-Jones, Saunders Medical Publishing, Sycom for card pack programs.
- Generated $6.2 million in revenue through card pack advertising programs.
- Counseled clients with respect to direct marketing advertising programs.

References available on request

Leroy Williams

122 Pike Drive, Denver, Colorado 80236
Cellular: (303) 555-4428

Objective

To obtain employment as a junior systems analyst

Education

University of California at Los Angeles
B.S. Computer Science, 1996

Technical Expertise

Hardware: IBM PC/XT, IBM PC/AT, HP 3000, Leading Edge-XT
Software: CLIPPER; DBASE II AND III, POWER C, MPAS, PC-DOS

Background

9/98 - 9/00
- Appeared on five episodes of "Days of Our Lives"
- Booked two national TV commercials
- Wrote national TV commercial for Motrin IB
- Designed and implemented a computer system for the University of California's Engineering Department

8/96 - 1998
Diadem Optical Systems, Los Angeles, CA
Softwear Engineer
- Responsible for detailed specifications, designs, implementation, and maintenance of the software that controls and acquires data from a real-time experimental laser system. Key duties included providing software specification reviews for internal and external audiences.
- Integrated and implemented hardware/software system to acquire data from different sensor channels.
- Implemented complex mathematical algorithms used to control the laser system and to provide diagnostic information.

References available upon request

ELLEN WHITTMAN

145 W. BROAD STREET • CONCORD, NEW HAMPSHIRE 03301 • CELLULAR: (603) 555-7683

OBJECTIVE

Senior position in financial management and analysis

ACCOMPLISHMENTS

American Cancer Society, volunteer
- Counseled women with breast cancer on treatment options, clinical trials, and cancer-related services in local areas
- Organized fund-raising activities that resulted in an increase of 2.3 million dollars for breast cancer research
- Lobbied to expand political action on women's health issues
- Facilitated a group for cancer survivors to support adjusting to life following cancer treatment
- Presented workshops on financial planning

PROFESSIONAL FINANCIAL MANAGEMENT EXPERIENCE

- Developed information systems to assess the present and future financial requirements of the firm
- Supervised 50 professional accountants and support personnel
- Expanded financial and economic policies that increased profits by 30 percent
- Established procedures to implement those policies
- Monitored and controlled the flow of cash receipts, disbursements, and financial instruments

EMPLOYMENT SUMMARY

Taylor Financial Group -- Concord, NH (1985 - 1998)
Amco Corporation -- Concord, NH (1978 - 1985)

EDUCATION

University of New Hampshire,
M.A., Accounting, 1977
B.A., Accounting, 1976

REFERENCES

Available upon request

MITCHELL MOORE

7862 Palm Lane
Hialeah, Florida 33010
Home: (305) 555-0896
Cell: (305) 555-7745

OBJECTIVE
  To utilize my legal knowledge and program development skills in a public relations or community service firm.

EDUCATION
  Fordham University Law School, New York, New York, J.D., 1973
  Florida State University, Tallahassee, Florida, B.A. History, 1970

  West Palm Beach Institute, West Palm Beach, Florida
  Volunteer/patient 1995 - 2000
  After completing this inpatient program in 1995, I volunteered to help design, run, and obtain financial backing for new programs to treat individuals and families confronted with alcoholism. My fund-raising activities resulted in a 40 percent expansion of services. We offer twelve-step guidance, stress management workshops, communications classes, education about alcoholism, family therapy, self-help groups, and continuing support. I have moved back to Hialeah but continue to facilitate support groups and attend AA on a regular basis. I am free of chemical dependency.

EMPLOYMENT EXPERIENCE
  KWN-TV
  Hollywood, Florida 1991 - 1995
  Handled all communications with the Federal Communications Commission. Prepared and filed license renewal applications, employment reports, and other documents required by the FCC on a regular basis. Researched and informed management of changing FCC regulations and their effect on our office procedures. Managed the acquisition of a local TV network.

  Derskowitz, Phillips, Schwartz, and Moore Esq.
  Orlando, Florida 1980 - 1990
  Specialized in contracts, wills, trusts, mortgages and titles.

  Motorola Incorporated
  Orlando, Florida 1973 - 1980
  Served as house counsel. Advised on questions concerning patents, government regulations, contracts, property interests, and collective bargaining agreements with union delegates

REFERENCES ARE ENCLOSED

Linda DiMartino
1700 Ocean Avenue #12A
Brooklyn, NY 11232
(718) 555-7651

Volunteer Experience

ASSOCIATION FOR THE PREVENTION OF CRUELTY TO ANIMALS,
12/98 - PRESENT.
Conceived, developed, and implemented a computerized filing system.
Designed an outreach program that resulted in a 45 percent increase in adoptions. Interviewed, evaluated, and recommended applicants wishing to adopt a pet.

Employment Experience

SENNITI, KRUMBERG, AND JONES, LEGAL SECRETARY, 3/71 - 5/98.
Prepared legal documents such as summonses, complaints, motions, and subpoenas. Assisted with legal research. Investigated cases. Updated material in the law library. Maintained escrow accounts. Composed correspondence and reports from briefing on subject and purpose. Initiated office procedures that saved time and money.
Promoted to Executive Legal Secretary, 1978.

Skills

Hardware: Standard PC
Self-starter. Accomplish goals effectively and efficiently.

Activities

Active member of the National Association of Legal Secretaries.
Elected secretary for Mediterranean Towers co-op board.
Active member of National Wildlife Association.

References

Available upon request.

Amanda Sandlewood

297 West 24th Street
Cheyenne, WY 82001
(307) 555-2148
A_Sandlewood@xxx.com

Professional Objective

A position as manager in a human resources firm.

Achievements

1997 - present
- Elected president of the P.T.A. for five consecutive years.
- Organized outreach activities that increased membership by 25 percent.
- Organized fund-raising activities that increased revenue by 15 percent each year.
- Established after-school activities such as chess classes and reading groups.
- Hired specialists in various fields, such as music, for the after-school activities.
- Coordinated all activities and meetings of the P.T.A.

Professional Experience

Manager, customer support, American Express, Cheyenne, WY
1991 - 1997
Achievements:
- Managed a budget of 1.5 million dollars.
- Responsible for hiring customer-sensitive and supportive employees.
- Designed employee development workshops to promote quality of service approach toward customer relations.
- Developed a team system approach for handling difficult problems.
- Managed a staff of 25 professionals.
- Assisted in the development of a new mail-order sales approach.
- Implemented procedures to increase communication between departments.

Customer Service Representative
1990 - 1991
Achievements:
- Assisted customers by resolving complaints.
- Introduced new methods of settling disputes.
- Received Employee of the Year award.

Education

University of Wyoming, Laramie, Wyoming
- M.A. Business and Marketing, 1990
- B.A. Psychology, 1989

References

Available upon request

YOLANDA WILLIAMS

152 Alexandria Street, Apt. 3W
Washington, DC 20013
Home: (202) 555-9897
Pager: (202) 555-3363

OBJECTIVE
A part-time nursing position to assist a physician in private practice

EDUCATION
BSN, University of Richmond, Richmond, Virginia 1952
Post-RN training program for nurse midwives, District of Columbia
General Hospital, Washington, DC 1974

SUMMARY OF QUALIFICATIONS
Forty years experience in nursing care.
Duties included:
- Assessment and development of treatment plans.
- Participation in the patients' convalescence and rehabilitation.
- Provision of health maintenance, nutritional information, and care for pregnant women.
- Evaluation of the progress of labor.
- Routine labor and deliveries.
- Teaching courses in Lamaze.
- Provision of continuous post-operative pain-management procedures.

ACCOMPLISHMENTS
Established Lamaze classes at District of Columbia General Hospital
- Supervised a staff of 7 RNs, 4 LANs, and 10 nursing aids.
- Developed, implemented, and managed convalescence and rehabilitation programs in Richmond Community Hospital that resulted in a 35 percent increase in government and private funding.

EMPLOYMENT
District of Columbia General Hospital, Washington, DC 2/74 - 7/93
Retired in 1993 and traveled extensively throughout Europe
Richmond Community Hospital, Richmond, Virginia, 8/52 - 2/74

References are enclosed

KERI KAPLAN

16 Sydney Road
Fairfax, Virginia 22030
(703) 555-9980
Keri_Kaplan@xxx.com

OBJECTIVE

To secure employment as an administrative assistant in a company that will benefit from my strong creative and management skills.

MANAGERIAL EXPERIENCE

CRABTREE CRAFTS SHOP, SHENANDOAH NATIONAL PARK, VA 1996 - 2001
MASTER JEWELER/ PARTNER

Created silver jewelry, which I then sold from Crabtree Crafts Shop. I became a partner in 1990 and was responsible for recruiting, training, and supervising employees. I developed an advertising campaign program that increased revenues by $15,000/month. Produced a computerized book-keeping system.

ADMINISTRATIVE EXPERIENCE

TREAT HARVEY INVESTMENT GROUP, FAIRFAX, VA 1985 - 1996
ADMINISTRATIVE ASSISTANT

Devised and implemented new office procedures. Identified and resolved problems within the organization. Composed correspondence regarding policies and procedures. Wrote numerous speeches for CEOs. Prepared reports and replied to correspondence.

COMPUTER BACKGROUND

Microsoft Suite including Excel, Access, Word, and PowerPoint
Versed in various E-mail packages and online resources

EDUCATION

Hollins College, Roanoke, VA
B.A. English, 1984

MEMBERSHIPS

National Association for Women in Business

References available on request.

Mia Merriweather

20 Cedar Pines Lane
Logan, Utah 84322
(801) 555-2956

• OBJECTIVE

To return to a challenging position as a music therapist.

• EDUCATION

Utah State, Logan, Utah
Bachelor of Science Degree in Recreation Therapy 1987

• VOLUNTEER EXPERIENCE

1996 - present
- Assisted in the affairs of the *Navajo Economic Opportunity Bureau*.
- Established a local community development program.
- Designed projects to improve housing conditions and availability.
- Developed strategies and campaigned to increase funding for medical care and educational facilities.
- Lobbied and achieved funding for a community-based alcoholism treatment program.
- Worked directly with Navajo youth, enrolling them in counseling and job training programs.
- Promoted a successful food drive for the Navajo community.

• PROFESSIONAL EXPERIENCE

Salt Lake Rehabilitation Center, Salt Lake City, Utah
Recreational Therapist, 1987 - 1996
- Sought to reverse the negative effects of disabilities by building self-esteem through various activities
- Developed individual treatment plans.
- Organized and coordinated a yearly arts fair in which all clients participated.
- Presented four plays a year in the community theater. Acting and backstage activities conducted solely by our clients.
- Supervised three recreational therapists in charge of scheduling board game and sports events.
- Supervised two therapists who managed the leisure activities program.
- Encouraged family members to participate in treatment.
- Received Mayor's Award for Achievement in the area of Community Service, 1990 and 1991.

References available on request

Jay Vasquez

290 Hollywood Boulevard
Los Angeles, California 90063
(213) 555-1226

Career Objective

A position in security in a company that will profit from my extensive experience in law enforcement.

Career History

Twenty-five years experience in police work. Moved up the ranks to detective after only four years on the force.

Skills and Accomplishments

- Conflict resolution skills.
- Worked with disadvantaged youth in South Central High Schools.
- Excellent social and communication skills that enabled me to ease tensions and promote verbal interchange.
- Ability to supervise and educate.
- Received several mayoral, community, and distinguished service awards.
- Sharpshooter.

Experience

1986 - 1999: Youth Officer, George Washington High School, Los Angeles, CA
              Martin Luther King High School, Los Angeles, CA
1981 - 1986: Special Agent, U.S. Drug Enforcement Administration
1978 - 1981: Homicide Detective, 12th precinct, Los Angeles, CA
1974 - 1978: Patrolman, 12th precinct, Los Angeles, CA

Education

FBI Academy, Quantico, VA. Specialized training in drug enforcement
B.A. Psychology, University of Los Angeles, Los Angeles, CA, 1976

References available on request

HAROLD OVERBAND

1009 Buck Drive
Huntsville, Alabama 35804

Home: (205) 555-3928
Cellular: (205) 555-0091

GOAL

To return to a challenging career in sales and marketing.

EDUCATION

M.B.A. Columbia University, New York, NY, 1972
B.A. Business Administration, University of Alabama at Birmingham, 1970

VOLUNTEER EXPERIENCE

1991 - 1998
Dean Ornish Program, New York, NY
After retiring due to illness, I successfully completed Dr. Ornish's program and trained to help others. I taught classes in meditation, nutrition, and food preparation.

- Ameliorated the need for surgery for most people attending the course.
- Introduced new concepts that became part of the coursework and were presented in Dr. Ornish's new book.
- Reversed my condition to one of perfect health.

WORK EXPERIENCE

1988 - 1991
BRUER ENVELOPE CO., Huntsville, Alabama, Sales and Marketing Manager

- Initiated an aggressive sales campaign and new marketing strategies.
- Contracted 35 new corporate accounts.
- Increased sales from $195,000 to $275,000 over a five-year period.
- Introduced an innovative customer service unit.
- Altered company image by stressing quality products.

1972 - 1988
SAMSONITE LUGGAGE, Birmingham, Alabama, Sales Manager

- Supervised 20 regional salesmen and women.
- Established a novel training program that stimulated sales personnel to generate 55 percent increase in business after the first year of its inception.
- Increased new accounts with dealers and distributors to more than 100.
- Surveyed needs of customers and developed successful pricing strategies.

MEMBER of the International Sales and Marketing Executive Committee

References available on request

Yetta Lewin

3122 High Road
Warwick, Rhode Island 0288
(401) 555-7766
Yetta_Lewin@xxx.com

Education

J.D., Harvard Law School, 1998
Graduated top 10%

B.A. History, Harvard University, 1995
G.P.A. 3.8

Skills

Raised four children.
- Developed tolerance, patience, and negotiating skills.
- Learned to develop strategies to achieve goals.
- Exercised sound judgment in all areas of child rearing.
- Developed useful time-management skills.

As wife to the city comptroller, I accomplished the following:
- Created a foundation that funded three arts centers for the handicapped.
- Established a volunteer theater program in Warwick General Hospital.
- Gained financial assistance for breast cancer support organization.
- Founded the Warwick, RI division of The Breast Cancer Coalition.
- Organized funding activities for the Coalition.
- Instituted a yearly walk-a-thon for the Susan G. Komen Breast Cancer Foundation.

Registration

Member of the Bar Association. Licensed to practice in Rhode Island and Massachusetts.

References are enclosed

JOE CHU

c/o Midwestern State University
3400 Taft Boulevard
Wichita Falls, Texas 76308
(817) 555-6515

OBJECTIVE

To obtain a challenging entry-level position in an environmental protection agency.

EDUCATION

Currently a student at Midwestern State University
M.S. candidate, Geology
Projected date of graduation: June 2002
G.P.A. 4.0

Dissertation topic: Engineering Improvements for Waste Disposal Sites in Warm Climates

University of Taipei, Taipei, Taiwan
B.A. Mechanical Engineering, 1990

WORK EXPERIENCE

7/96 - 7/97
Haung Design Group Inc., Taipei, Taiwan, Project Engineer
- Three years experience in working with mechanical systems within commercial projects
- Developed construction portion of architectural designs.
- Directed numerous multimillion-dollar design projects of commercial structures.
- Created labor-saving strategies that resulted in downsizing of workforce by 25 percent.
- Responsible for quality control.

8/90 - 7/96
Susing Construction Co., Taipei, Taiwan, Junior Engineer
- Researched and developed mechanical systems related to the construction of commercial facilities.
- Responsible for resolving technical problems related to failing mechanical systems.
- Analyzed and tested heat transport systems.

ADDITIONAL SKILLS

DOS/VSE, Cobol, Basic, Fortran, CICS, Pascal, C Plus

REFERENCES

Furnished on request

BECKY HORN

190 University Avenue • Honolulu, Hawaii 96822
Home: 808-555-9261 • B_Horn39@xxx.com

GOAL
To re-enter my chosen field as a Clinical Dietitian in a private facility

BACKGROUND
1993 - present:
- Established a profitable clothing business which was operated from my home.
- Increased earnings to $25,000 last year.
- Presented tag and garage sales.
- Organized neighborhood street fairs.
- Sold clothing to vendors on consignment.
- Conducted fashion shows in several restaurants for tourists that increased sales 50 percent.

EMPLOYMENT
1970 - 1993:
MERCY HOSPITAL, MINNEAPOLIS, MINNESOTA
Clinical Dietitian
Major responsibilities & achievements:
- Managed the planning of all meals in the facility
- Promoted to Administrative Dietitian and supervised a staff of 30 employees.
- Designed and conducted staff workshops to educate groups on the nutritional analysis of food and healthful preparation.
- Assessed the nutritional needs of patients; planned and implemented a program to meet their needs.
- Developed community nutritional training programs.
- Modified the typical institutional dietary menu.

EDUCATION
M.S. Nutrition, University of Nevada, Reno, Nevada, 1969
B.S. Food Service Administration, University of Miami, Coral Gables, Florida, 1966

ACCREDITATION
American Dietetic Association

References are enclosed

NINA MAZZOLA

2017 Menaul N.E.
Albuquerque, New Mexico
(505) 555-9804
Mazzola@xxx.com

OBJECTIVE   A position in International Relations in a Western European Agency

EDUCATION   University of Oregon, Eugene, Oregon
B.A. International Relations, *cum laude*, 1982

SKILLS/ACCOMPLISHMENTS

- Fluent in Spanish and Italian
- Service-oriented, tactful, benevolent
- Work independently, under pressure, flexible hours
- Certified in CPR
- Negotiated innovative work rules with airline executives
- Secured the release of innocent prisoners in New Mexico
- Received four Superior Service awards
- Worked in Spain, assisting foreigners in emergency situations and obtaining legal counsel for them
- Resolved complex cases of consular policy
- Settled disputes with special interest groups
- Developed a public relations campaign and achieved unprecedented working relationships with government employees
- Won support for U.S. foreign policy initiatives

WORK HISTORY

1994 - present
VOLUNTEER, Centurion Ministries, Albuquerque, New Mexico
This prison advocacy group investigates claims of innocence and works for the release of prisoners it finds credible.

1983 - 1994
FOREIGN SERVICE OFFICER, Department of State
Consular officer, 1983 - 1992
Political officer, 1992 - 1994

1982 - 1983
STUDENT, Foreign Service Institute

1975 - 1978
FLIGHT ATTENDANT, Delta Airlines

REFERENCES AVAILABLE UPON REQUEST

CARL KLEIN, M.D.
2401 LIGHTHOUSE AVENUE
MONTEREY, CALIFORNIA 93950
HOME: 408-555-8885
PAGER: 408-555-3112

GOAL

To obtain employment in a major medical center

EDUCATION

1990 Georgetown University School of Medicine, Washington, D.C.
1986 University of San Diego, California, B.S. Biology
G.P.A. 4.0

VOLUNTEER EXPERIENCE

1998 - 2000 VISTA UNIVERSITY, Soweto, South Africa

Worked with the Deputy Minister of culture and the faculty of Vista to establish outreach programs in health, nutrition, and prenatal care. Created and managed several local walk-in clinics, and supervised 35 professionals in Alexandra and Chiawello townships under the auspices of The College of Medicine of South Africa. Received a part-time appointment at the University of Pretoria, Dept. of Family Practice, postgraduate training program. Contributor to the *Journal of the Association of South Africa.*

WORK EXPERIENCE

1995 - 1998 D.C. General Hospital
1990 - 1995 Richmond University Medical Center, Richmond, VA,
internship and residence.
Specialty in Family Medicine

MEMBERSHIPS

South African Academy of Family Practice/Primary Care
South African Medical and Dental Council
Medical Association of South Africa
Department of Family Practice of Virginia
The D.C. College of Medicine

Eugene Louie

1254 N. 11th Street
Beaumont, Texas 77702
Cellular: (409) 555-8345

OBJECTIVE

To offer my expertise in business matters on a consulting basis

1994 - present
Business consultant -- VOLUNTEER RETIRED EXECUTIVES
Beaumont, Texas

SELECTED ACCOMPLISHMENTS

- Cofounded Global Plastics Corporation 1950
- Traded in raw materials and machinery
- Instrumental in expanding operations into Central and South America
- Formed affiliates in 1960
- Induced Board of Directors to expand into Australia and Canada
- Sold Company 1970 for $30 million
- Acquired Inter-Ocean Plastics 1971
- Increased stock buyback to 12.5 million shares
- Focused on core strengths and took an $86 million charge against earnings for costs relating to downsizing
- Restructured and sold off certain manufacturing operations producing an annual savings of $7 million
- Founded and chaired Plastics Association of America (a Washington trade group)

MEMBERSHIPS

National Businessmen's Association

REFERENCES

Available on request

Sample Cover Letters

This chapter contains many sample cover letters for people pursuing a wide variety of jobs and careers in the field of law, or who have had experience in this field in the past.

There are many different styles of cover letters in terms of layout, level of formality, and presentation of information. These samples also represent people with varying amounts of education and work experience. Choose one cover letter or borrow elements from several different cover letters to help you construct your own.

REGINALD D. DAWSON
4800 Johnson Plank Road • Albuquerque, NM 87819
505-555-4889

May 20, 20____

Michelle Vance, Supervisor
Applewood Sports Therapy Association
3500 Applewood Blvd.
Albuquerque, NM 87822

Dear Ms. Vance:

Please accept the enclosed resume as an application for employment
with your organization. I learned of the available opening through Dr.
John Weber, Dean of the School of Sports Medicine, University of New
Mexico. He suggested I contact you and apply for the position using him
as a personal reference.

As you will notice on my resume, I have a diverse background in
alternative healing procedures training, all of which I have successfully
used in my internship program at the University of New Mexico. Aware
of Applewood Sports Therapy protocol, I feel I would make a valuable
contribution as a member of your staff. My professional beliefs are in
total synchronization with your policies and practices.

I look forward to meeting with you and discussing my qualifications.
I feel we can both benefit from my employment as part of your team
organization. Please contact me at your earliest convenience.

Sincerely,

Reginald D. Dawson

Jane M. Michaels
12 Harvard Avenue, Apt. G
Reno, NV 72367
Cellular: 702-555-9956
Home: 702-555-7384

March 30, 20___

Mr. William Reilly
Reno Tourist Office
534 Park Avenue
Reno, NV 72359

Dear Mr. Reilly:

I am writing in regard to your advertisement in the Sunday edition of the *Reno Star Ledger* on the available position of Assistant Accountant at the Reno Tourist Office.

As an accounting clerk at Sam's Club department store in Blairsville, I have demonstrated responsibility and dependability. I am reliable, detail-oriented, creative, and extremely well organized. I have gained knowledge and experience in office procedures through my full-time position in accounts receivable. I am confident that I would be an asset in the position of Assistant Accountant within your organization.

I have enclosed my resume for your review and would appreciate the opportunity to discuss my qualifications with you. I may be contacted at my cellular or home telephones at the numbers listed above. I look forward to hearing from you in the very near future.

Sincerely,

Jane M. Michaels

Sandra L. Gardiner

81 Huntington Lane • Buffalo, NY 11456 • (716) 555-7849

February 25, 20____

Robert Grimm
Sales Manager
Chase Chevrolet, Inc.
23 West Market Street
Buffalo, NY 11473

Dear Mr. Grimm:

I am writing to you in response to the sales position opening advertised in the *Buffalo Record*.

As you will see from the enclosed resume, I possess the necessary years of skill and experience for the available sales position. I thoroughly enjoy working with people and possess excellent communications skills, as well as a pleasant personality. I am a very organized and self-motivated individual. I am sure I would be a credit to your firm.

I would greatly appreciate an interview at your earliest convenience to further discuss my qualifications for this position. I look forward to hearing from you.

Thank you for your consideration.

Sincerely,

Sandra L. Gardiner

Marie M. Patterson
33 Wrigley Avenue, Apt. 22
Hyattstown, MD 22314

12 January 20_____

John M. Constanov
President
Cedar Grove Condominiums
300 Cedar Grove Avenue
Olney, MD 22176

Dear Mr. Constanov:

As an experienced office manager and administrative employee, I am applying for the position of office manager of the Cedar Groves Condominiums Association.

An owner and board member, Mrs. Cecilia Wentworth has advised me of the available position. She has suggested that I first contact you in regard to the available opening, as you are making a selection of candidates for the governing board's review.

I believe the abilities I possess may be of use to the condominium's association. I have gained considerable knowledge and have enhanced my management skills throughout my professional history. I consider myself to be an effective communicator and possess excellent organizational skills, which I feel are my greatest strengths.

I am submitting the enclosed resume for your consideration and evaluation. I am looking forward to meeting with you and the condominium board to discuss my qualifications, as I realize my appointment would be based on a ballot selection. I look forward to hearing from you in the near future.

Sincerely yours,

Marie M. Patterson

SUZANNE M. GEORGE

7919 Ragland Drive
Girard, OH 44484
216/555-5647

April 17, 20____

Clarence Jansen
Station Manager
WCAK Television
1 Enterprise Way
Akron, Ohio 44223

Dear Mr. Jansen:

In reference to our telephone conversation this afternoon, please find my resume enclosed for review for the news anchor person position. Having been employed as a Junior Reporter with the WKBN television news team in Youngstown for three years, my experience has been thorough on and off the camera.

My background in journalism has given me a foundation to be factual and personable, traits that have set me apart from just reporting the news. I am confident that I can make a vital contribution to your news team. If you will give me the opportunity, I will prove that to you and the WCAK viewing audience.

I look forward to the opportunity to discuss my qualifications with you in a personal interview. Thank you for your time and consideration.

Sincerely,

Suzanne M. George

NATASHA L. WOODBINE
21101 Locust Valley Rd.
Marlburg, TN 37223
615/555-3684

March 29, 20____

Sarah Westmore
Office Manager
Barnes Office Supply Co.
Regal and Park Ave.
Nashville, TN 37399

Dear Ms. Westmore:

I am writing to inform you of my qualifications and interest in the secretarial position available with your company. I saw the position advertised on the Nashville Cablevision "Job Opportunity Notebook" segment.

I am a highly motivated individual with a desire for achievement. My skills and abilities coupled with my enthusiasm and ambition make me a strong candidate for employment within your organization.

Details of my academic and employment background are provided on the enclosed resume. I would be happy to provide any additional information that you would require. An interview to discuss my qualifications would be greatly appreciated.

Thank you for your time and consideration.

Sincerely,

Natasha L. Woodbine

Horoko Kimura

111 Southwest Blvd.
East Providence, RI 02777
401/555-4871

March 26, 20____

Patrick M. Welshans
Vice President
Superior Mortgage Brokers, Inc.
Accounting Department
12 Marginal Road Highway
Providence, RI 02789

Dear Mr. Welshans:

I am responding to your advertisement in the *Providence Herald* for the position of staff accountant. My previous experience, as detailed in my resume, highlights my accounting career. My abilities in the accounting field would be a great asset to your company.

My former position with Rankin, Smith and Hightower Investment Corp., Inc. was built upon a successful foundation that graduated from the position of Junior Accountant to a Senior Staff Accounting position. However, when the company moved out of state, I felt that it would be in my best interest to complete my studies at the University of Providence and attain my Bachelor of Science degree in Accounting.

Now that I have graduated, I am eager to continue in my chosen field. I would like to discuss my career objective with you in regard to the position now available in your company. I will telephone you next week to set up an appointment at your convenience. I am looking forward to meeting with you and discussing this available position.

Sincerely,

Horoko Kimura

RENA A. MADISON
1412 Bittersweet Court
Roanoke, VA 23059

May 30, 20____

Constance M. Bingham
Clarice Fashions, Ltd.
230 Van Buren Highway
Roanoke, VA 23066

Dear Ms. Bingham:

Your advertisement for a seamstress in the May issue of *Fabric World* interested me greatly, and I would like to be considered an applicant for this position.

While at the Lisa Martell School of Clothing Design in Roanoke, I obtained many skills that I believe would be of great value to your company. I have successfully completed courses in pattern design, pattern grading, and pattern making. I am considered an excellent seamstress by the number of clients I have sewn for throughout the past ten years. Although sewing was only a hobby for the last two years, I would now like to reapply my skills in the business world.

I would like to meet with you and elaborate on my credentials and abilities. I would be more than happy to have you examine some of my creations and artistry.

The resume I have enclosed is just a sample of my experience. I will call you early next week to set up an appointment for an interview. Thank you for your time and consideration.

Sincerely,

Rena A. Madison

JOHN P. RODGERS
3478 Harmon Cove Rd.
Lincoln, NE 68990
402/555-9956

July 10, 20____

Albert M. Moore
General Merchandising Company
1008 Market St.
Lincoln, NE 68990

Dear Mr. Moore:

Please review my qualifications for the current job opening in your organization. I believe they are well suited to the job description you have advertised. My background in clerical administration includes, but is not limited to, all the requirements you have outlined for this position.

Although my resume summarizes my last four years work experience, I have eight years total experience in the clerical/administrative area. This position with your company would give me the opportunity to continue in the field in which I have successfully performed professionally in my military career.

I would appreciate the opportunity to discuss this position in more detail in an interview at your convenience.

Sincerely,

John P. Rodgers

Robert Berger
576 Main Street
Hartford, CT 06088
203-555-9243

Linda Jensen
CNBC
3657 Lemoine Avenue
Fort Lee, NJ 07024

Dear Ms. Jensen:

Jonas Bernstein told me about your search for a producer of documentaries. I would like to apply for that position.

I have worked as an associate producer for "The MacNeil-Lehrer Report," "CBS Reports," "48 Hours," "West 57th Street," and "20/20." Some highlights of my career are interviews with Prince Charles, Abolhassan Bani-Sadr, Carlos Salinas de Gortari, and Gerry Adams.

I have a master's degree in Film and a Bachelor of Arts in English Literature. Both were earned at New York University.

Enclosed is my resume detailing my work and volunteer experience. I spent this past year recovering from an injury that resulted from an automobile accident, and I am anxious to get back to work.

Thank you for your time and consideration. I look forward to meeting you.

Sincerely,

Robert Berger

JULIA M. JOHNSDOTTIR

222 Barnaby Ave.
Wheatland, PA 19451
215-555-1234

April 20, 20__

Michael Flanagan, D.D.S.
Keystone Dental Clinic
80-34 Sunrise Highway
Pembroke, PA 19444

Dear Dr. Flanagan:

I am writing to you on the recommendation of my dentist, Dr. Gerald Hotchkiss. He suggested I send you my resume in anticipation of the Dental Hygienist position that will be available next month in your clinic.

I graduated from Oldenburg School of Dental Hygiene in 1993, however, my experience as a Dental Assistant was between 1993 and 1996. Raising a family put my career on hold, but since I had always enjoyed my work in dentistry, I enhanced my background and pursued my goal. I am now ready to devote myself to a full-time career as a Dental Hygienist.

My dedication to the field is evident in my volunteer work with the Pennsylvania Dental Association. I would like to have an appointment with you to discuss my qualifications for this position. I look forward to hearing from you.

Sincerely,

Julia M. Johnsdottir

CALDER LAWSON
44 Wilson Drive
Newark, New Jersey 07030
(201) 555-8794

Mr. Jack McSheehan
Columbia Music Corporation
114 East 34th Street
New York, NY 10016

Dear Mr. McSheehan:

I saw your ad for Executive Vice President in the *Baltimore Sun Times* on May 2, 2001, and I am writing to request an interview.

I rose through the ranks of Freeman department stores and became president in 1981. I led the company into an expansion program and in 1994 negotiated a merger with Mays department stores. I remained the vice president of the Mays company until 1999 when I retired due to an illness from which I have completely recovered.

My interests and involvement in music inspired me to consider your company as a prospective employer. I request an opportunity to discuss the opening and my background in greater detail.

Sincerely,

Calder Lawson

Linda Powell • 4 Rutland St. • Chicago, IL 60603

June 4, 20_____

Bob Lenny
Hansen Foods
34 Board St.
Chicago, IL 60601

Dear Mr. Lenny,

Your classified advertisement in the *Tribune* was of interest to me. The knowledge and experience I gained with my twenty years experience at Eastern Telecom closely matches your requirements.

As my resume indicates, I have had progressively more responsibility in the field of Human Resources. I concentrated in but did not limit myself to, the areas of compensation, manpower planning, and benefits. I have utilized my strong analytical skills in many areas.

During my experience I have exhibited excellent interpersonal skills and strong computer knowledge, been a solid team player, and utilized both verbal and written communications skills to all levels of employees and management.

I look forward to having the opportunity talk further with you in the near future.

Best wishes,

Linda Powell

Shakima Davis
675 San Diego, California 92101
(619) 555-7834

Mr. Don Kaplan
The Star Ledger
1936 Nimitz Blvd.
San Diego, California 92106

Dear Mr. Kaplan:

I am writing in application for the position of Associate Editor which was advertised in *Sunday's Ledger*. My previous experience includes employment at D.C. Comics as Junior Editor, and BAI radio in NY as staff comedy writer. I have also written syndicated comic strips and have enclosed them for your review. Two of my books for young readers, *Outstanding Playoffs* (1997) and *Sport Stories* (2000) were published by Four Winds/Macmillan, which I would be happy to forward to you at your request.

I have spent the past two years traveling and now wish to return to work. I hope I can have the opportunity to meet with you to discuss the qualities I can bring to the editorial profession.

Sincerely,

Shakima Davis

JOHN FITZGERALD

2 Gotham Street
Detroit, MI 54663

July 7, 20____

David Schuster
Gotham Industries
445 Milk Street
Detroit, MI 55677

Dear Mr. Schuster,

I am writing you concerning your openings in customer service and sales. As my resume outlines, I have had extensive experience in these functions. Some of my accomplishments include the following:

• Directed development of a Fortune 500 company's five-year strategic plan.
• Developed and presented marketing proposals to the corporate executive committee.
• Conducted a market research study on the commercialization of catalysts manufactured in space for a major aerospace firm.
• Created and managed the customer service department for a major manufacturer.
• Designed operational flow charts, tracking systems, and productivity measurements.

My background has been very successful in many diverse and challenging environments. I look forward to meeting you in person to discuss how my talents can lead to superior results for you. I will call you next week to arrange a convenient time.

Sincerely,

John Fitzgerald

WILLIAM R. BABBIO

Ms. Amy Jones
AT&T
P.O. Box 8795
Columbus, GA 31908-9563

Dear Ms. Jones:

I am writing to follow up on our telephone conversation on Thursday in which we discussed AT&T's need for a chief operating officer. As we discussed, I am currently completing my volunteer Vista assignment in New Mexico and will be arriving in Georgia on July 3rd. As chief operating officer with MCI, I was the key deal-maker and responsible for expanding into new markets such as computer maintenance. I was also the chief negotiator in the acquisition of Tele-Communications Inc., the nation's largest cable company.

I am enclosing a resume for your review and hope to hear from you soon.

Sincerely,

William R. Babbio
555 Scott Avenue,
Farmington, New Mexico 87401

Enclosure

ANDY KARLSON

735 Winston Way • Raleigh, NC 44943 • (919) 555-0285

REGENERON
8566 Main Street
Charlotte, NC 28255

To Whom It May Concern:

This letter is in response to an ad placed in the *Charlotte News* on November 3, 2001. I am writing to inquire about the position and to tell you something about myself.

Prior to my retirement in 1999, I served as assistant research scientist, first at the National Heart Institute and then at Washington University's School of Medicine. I really miss what I've been doing for most of my life and would welcome an opportunity to join your distinguished research facility.

If you need further information after reading my resume, please do not hesitate to contact me.

Sincerely,

Andy Karlson

JOSEPH K. McANDREWS

4352 Genesse Street • Buffalo, NY 14225 • 716-555-9576

Reverend Kevin O'Conner
Canisuis College
3654 Main Street
Buffalo, NY 14203

Dear Reverend O'Conner:

I am very interested in applying for the position you have available for Director of the university's counseling center. I am a Jesuit priest and received my doctorate in psychology from Yale in 1985. I served as chairman of the Psychology Department at Georgetown University for many years and presided over the American Catholic Psychological Association from 1993 to 1999.

I have spent the last three years recovering from an illness of which I am now completely cured. I spent that time productively by writing articles that were published in professional journals, and I contributed chapters to several books.

Reverend Keegan, Associate Professor in your math department, informed me of the position in the counseling center, and I would greatly welcome an opportunity to meet with you. Please feel free to call me at your convenience. I look forward to hearing from you.

Sincerely,

Joseph McAndrews

Ron Lenhardt
7456 E. 7th Street
Omaha, Nebraska 51501

October 7, 20____

Mr. Leon Williams
Solar Age Genesis
3434 Abbott Drive
Omaha, Nebraska 68110

Dear Mr. Williams:

I am eager to pursue a position as a Senior Industrial Engineer
with Solar Age Genesis and I have enclosed a copy of my
resume for your review. I have spent 25 years working as an
Engineer for Solar Dimensions and retired in 1999.

I have greatly enjoyed the volunteer work I have done with
PAL, but I feel strongly motivated to return to my profession.
My areas of expertise have been in innovative designs, cost and
personnel reduction, and equipment justification.

I would appreciate the opportunity to discuss any openings
you may have in my field, and I look forward to meeting you.

Sincerely,

Ron Lenhardt

Norman Kerstman
737 Summit Drive
Portland, OR 97208
503-555-2534

May 4, 20_____

Ms. Jennifer Ross
Personnel Director
Lehman Brothers
325 Hollywood Boulevard
Los Angeles, California 90063

Dear Ms. Ross:

I enjoyed speaking with you last Monday about the merger-and-acquisition specialist position available at Lehman Brothers. I am certain that my employment at your company would be an asset. When I worked for Kohlberg, Katz and Roberts I completed two of the nation's largest leveraged buyouts: the acquisition of the Beatrice Companies and RJR Nabisco Inc. When I worked at Drexel in the mid-nineties I earned a substantial bonus each year as a result of my efforts.

For the last several years I have worked as an independent money manager and spent most of my free time doing volunteer work, but I now feel the urge to return to the excitement of negotiating big deals. I can say with certainty that I will continue to be successful in this field and look forward to discussing the possibility of working for Lehman Brothers.

Sincerely,

Norman Kerstman